£4-50

HELPING SICK CHILDREN PLAY

Nature, so our reasoning mind tells us, could just as easily have given her children all those useful functions of discharging superabundant energy, of relaxing after exertion, of training for the demands of life, of compensating for unfulfilled longings et cetera in the form of purely mechanical exercises and reactions. But no, she gave us play, with its tension, its mirth and its fun.

Huizinga: *Homo Ludens*

HELPING SICK CHILDREN PLAY

Barbara F. Weller RSCN, SRN, RNT

*Nursing Officer (Children's Division), Department of Health and Social Security,
United Kingdom*

with a foreword by
Frederic Brimblecombe CBE, MD, FRCP, DCH
Consultant Paediatrician, Royal Devon and Exeter Hospital

line drawings by Gillian Oliver

BAILLIÈRE TINDALL · LONDON

A BAILLIÈRE TINDALL book published by
Cassell Ltd,
35 Red Lion Square, London WC1R 4SG

and at Sydnev. Auckland, Toronto, Johannesburg

an affiliate of
Macmillan Publishing Co. Inc.
New York

First published 1980

ISBN 0 7020 0792 7

Printed in Great Britain by Spottiswoode Ballantyne Ltd, Colchester and London

British Library Cataloguing in Publication Data

Weller, Barbara Fiona
 Helping sick children play.
 1. Children—Hospital care
 2. Play therapy
 I. Title II. Oliver, Gillian
 618.9′2006′515   RJ242

 ISBN 0-7020-0792-7

Contents

Foreword

All children need to be enabled to play; this is as vital to them as love, food, warmth and protection from danger. If there is any man or woman still unconvinced that children in hospital have more need to be enabled to play than do children in their own homes, then let them read Maureen Oswin's book *The Empty Hours*.

Once this essential element in a child's life is appreciated, then comes the practical problem of how this enabling activity can be achieved in hospital surroundings; not just for one or two hours from Monday to Friday, for there are 168 hours in every week including the week-end hours as well as school and public holidays. For make no mistake about it, children do need adult help in order to be enabled to play.

Who then can supply this essential need? First and above all the parents, who know their children and who (provided they are given encouragement and confidence to continue their normal role whilst their child is in hospital) are the people who are usually best equipped to undertake it. Secondly specially appointed play staff who, whether they are paid or voluntary, should have received training for this work. Thirdly, nursery teachers and indeed teachers of children of school age; it is not easy to define the margins in the work of every good teacher where 'formal teaching' ends and where education through play begins. Fourthly, as this present book so clearly reveals, nurses have a marvellous potential contribution to make provided they are motivated, encouraged and trained to undertake it; not just State Registered Children's Nurses but all nurses whatever their training who are called upon to look after children.

Thank God that in the last twenty years there has been a transformation in attitudes about parents being allowed to be with their children in hospital for which the National Association for the Welfare of Children in Hospital must take a large share of the credit (although sadly there are still in the United Kingdom, even in some hospital wards where acutely sick children are nursed, entrenched pockets of resistance from some doctors and nurses to the policy of unrestricted visiting by parents). For mentally handicapped children in permanent hospital care (about 4500 of them in England and Wales) parental involvement is in most cases greatly reduced or totally non-existent. Here too the policy of home or community care with short stay periods of hospital care is beginning to transform the situation for our mentally handicapped children. But whether for short stay for the acutely ill or long stay for the handicapped it is usually impossible for the parent(s) to be with their child throughout every hour of their stay in hospital. It is the purpose of this book to ensure that those hours when the parents are absent or when the child is not asleep are not 'empty hours'.

The role of play staff whether paid or voluntary who have received appropriate training has been well described by Susan Harvey and Ann Hales Tooke in their book *Play in Hospital*. The number of hours that such staff spend on children's wards up and down the country varies enormously. When they are present they are invaluable to the children. Their second role is a teaching one for all the remaining staff, above all for the nurses who are the only people who are always on the ward for every hour of every day every week. Teachers similarly are present on children's wards for variable periods in different parts of the country and in various types of hospitals. I know that teachers spend many additional hours preparing their work. But at most the teacher is with the child for 40 hours of each week in term-time (that is for at most 36 weeks of the year). If you calculate the total number of hours, this works out at 1440 hours out of the total of 8760 hours in the year or put in another way 16.5% of the hours of the year. That leaves 83.5% of the hours when no teacher is present.

Hence this book! It is absolutely essential that nurses working with children in hospital should be motivated, encouraged and trained to enable children to play. As a paediatrician, I am convinced that for a sick child's recovery and well-being not only is technical medical and nursing care of the most skilled kind essential, but that the environment in which the child is cared for is also of the greatest importance. A positive approach to play activities is among the top priorities. This book is about the contribution that nurses can make to ensure that it is provided. It is in this spirit that I most strongly commend it.

December 1979   FREDERIC BRIMBLECOMBE

Preface

It is widely recognized that play is an essential part of a child's emotional and psychological development, and the child's need for play is as strong in sickness as in health. Play for a sick child at home is largely provided by the child's parents and family. In the children's ward, however, it is the nurse who, in addition to normal nursing care, must be aware of the sick child's need for play and must make suitable provision for it. Parents, hospital play workers and volunteers may all be involved, but it is the nurse who must assess her patient's condition and interpret his readiness for play.

This book is therefore written specifically for nurses but will, I hope, also be useful to parents and others involved in the care of sick children. I have attempted to give the reader an understanding of the nature and purpose of play, with particular reference to the needs of sick children. I have included a variety of suggestions and ideas for toys and play activities, in the hope that these will act as a springboard from which the reader may develop further ideas and activities.

A book of this kind cannot be written in isolation, and I should like especially to thank my nursing colleagues who gave me support and encouragement to proceed. Particular thanks must go to Miss D. MacCormack, Senior Nursing Officer, Children's Hospital, Sheffield; Miss B. Barchard, Chief Nursing Officer, and Sister J. McElnea of the Hospital for Sick Children, Great Ormond Street, London, who all gave some of their valuable time to read and comment on the manuscript. I would also like to thank Professor Brimblecombe for kindly agreeing to write the Foreword. Finally I should like to acknowledge the help received from Mrs P. Belson, and from the staff of Baillière Tindall.

February 1980   Barbara F. Weller

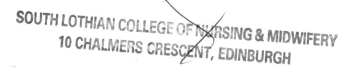

Acknowledgements

The author is grateful to the following, who have kindly supplied many of the illustrations which are included in the book: the Central Office of Information (pp. 3, 17, 79, 106 and 108); John Curtis (pp. 9, 11, 19, 21, 23, 83, 93 and 110); ESA Creative Learning (pp. 88 and 89); the Medical Illustration Department, Westminster Hospital Medical School, London (p. 101); Miss Kathleen Preston (pp. 39 and 70); and Constance E. King (p. 27).

Introduction

The needs of children vary considerably with age, but it is the nursing staff of a children's ward who set the pattern and standard of care provided for these children, and nurses who provide and plan this nursing care over every 24-hour period. As the provider of skilled care the nurse must recognize her responsibilities towards meeting the sick child's needs. Nursing care needs to be planned in co-operation with the other members of the ward team but also in partnership with the child's parents and family, in order that the child may maintain his normal relationships.

Playing is an essential characteristic of healthy childhood. It is the means whereby a child makes experiments and explores the world, sorting reality from fantasy. It is the way through which he can express to others and to himself, by re-enacting it again and again, what an experience has meant to him. Feelings of love, hope, fear and anger can be safely expressed in play and this contributes to mental health and stability. In hospital, children are often confused, frightened and angry. An adult with time to listen, or with younger ones, simply to hold and comfort them, may help children to manage such overwhelming feelings better. It is the person as much as any particular play activity that is so important at this stage. Play is deeply satisfying, especially when it comes spontaneously from the child himself or is initiated by an adult who understands its true purpose.

from *Guidelines for Play Volunteers Working with Children in Hospital in Acute Wards* (see Appendix 2)

Some health authorities now employ play staff who may be called play workers/leaders/ladies, some of whom will be specially trained, but as with every emerging group they bring differing experiences and skills to the provision of play. Their sole responsibility is to provide play within set hours for the children in the ward. However, if play is to be provided it should ideally be incorporated into total care and not isolated from the child's experience. Play opportunities may also be needed during twilight and night hours. Since the nursing staff are responsible for providing continuity of care, they should make definite provision in their planning for play opportunities and activities to take place at all times.

The play staff should be regarded as specialists, working together with nurses to meet special situations in much the same way as the nurse works with the dietitian. The nurse ensures that the meals provided are suited to the child's condition, age, needs, tastes and family influences (e.g. if vegetarian), and meet the body's requirements for metabolism, growth and development. However, if the child is suffering from severe diabetes or food allergy, skilled guidance and advice will be needed from the dietitian for a special diet. Nevertheless, the nurse is still ultimately responsible for ensuring that the child is able to eat and enjoy the diet provided.

Choosing toys, play materials and equipment appropriate to the child's age, condition and experiences requires understanding and care. Mia Kellmer Pringle, writing in her book *The Needs of Children*, suggests 'Ten Commandments for Child Care'. The fourth of these is 'encourage him to play in every way both by himself and with other children, exploring, imitating, constructing, pretending and creating'. Dr Kellmer Pringle recognizes that play 'provides a means of coping with and resolving conflicting emotions by allowing fantasy to override reality and logic'. This use of play is regarded as one of the prerequisites for healthy normal emotional and physical development. Today's children are tomorrow's parents and every aspect of child care needs to be looked at with this perspective in order to meet the child's basic requirements in a positive and encouraging way.

Nurses of sick children have in the past rather taken the play aspect of nursing care for granted. Originally it was the observations of James Robertson in *Young Children In Hospital* and of Eva Noble in *Play and the Sick Child* which drew our attention to the need to

---

Nursery nurses involved in the children's painting activity in the ward playroom.

reconsider what was then the generally accepted pattern of child care in hospitals. It is in the light of awareness that this book has been written. The intention is to provide nurses, nursery nurses, volunteers and others working with children in acute paediatric wards with a framework for play which will not only meet the developmental needs of the sick child, but will also promote his recovery and hasten his return to his family, school and normal environment.

The National Child Development Study has shown that no less than 43 per cent of the nation's children have been admitted to hospital by the age of seven years. Older children and adolescents are also admitted in considerable numbers. Such an experience for these children and their families is a matter of considerable importance. Their nursing care must allow for the continuation of normal childhood activities, play and hobbies.

It is with this knowledge in mind that the Joint Board of Clinical Nursing Studies has planned a course (Number 969) for nurses. The course is designed to promote understanding and a greater awareness of this dimension of the nursing role in the care of sick children.

In summary, the nurse needs to accept her responsibility to provide for and meet the child's basic needs for play. Play is an essential component of the child's life; as stated earlier, play is necessary for the child's normal healthy emotional and social development, enabling him to come to terms with conflicting emotions, fears and fantasies and to learn about and accept the world in which he lives. This is particularly important for the child in hospital who, in addition to being sick, is in a strange and threatening environment which he needs to come to terms with and incorporate into his total experience of growing up.

Participation in play introduces normality in a strange environment

Lessens the impact of pain and anxiety

Allows the child to work through feelings and fears so that hospitalization can become a positive experience

Yields results, recovery is faster and the in-patient stay is reduced

1. Play

Many adults regard play as a purposeless activity, a luxury indulged in by children or when mother wants them out of the way. It should, however, be considered as part of every child's natural inheritance and fundamental to the child's emotional, social and mental development. For young children play is work. Through play the child learns skills for living as well as learning to get on with others.

Play is not only confined to the human species but can also be observed in many animals. Behavioural zoologists believe that play increases the chances of survival for the animal, and for the group in their natural habitat. The more adaptable the animal, the more likely is it to engage in playful behaviour whilst young; for example, ants and bees show little evidence of play, whilst it is well reported and recognized amongst many primates and other mammals.

In play the animal relates to its environment and learns to communicate with members of the peer group whilst also learning from imitative group behaviour. Play also provides an acceptable opportunity for the young animal to test out new situations and feelings and to reinforce previously learned behaviour by repetition. Later, much of this playful behaviour can be observed in a more mature form during hunting, fighting and mating in which the value of play as a learning experience is evident. Play declines in adolescence and few mature animals indulge in play, except sometimes with their young.

UNDERSTANDING PLAY

Although play and all its functions are not fully understood various theories have been put forward. One of the earliest of these recognized the natural exuberance of much of children's play. The psychologist Herbert Spencer described play as an expenditure of surplus energy. Another psychologist in the nineteenth century suggested that the play of children reflects the course of evolution, the 'recapitulation' theory. Karl Groos saw the play of children as being instinctive preparation for adult life. The psychoanalytic concept put forward by Freud and others views play as a symbolic form of ideas and thoughts related to infant sexuality.

These theories explain only some of the components of play. The very complexity of the subject has led to many differing theories and explanations, none of which is entirely satisfactory in isolation. It would appear from the present evidence that play is a natural product of intellectual and emotional growth. But whether it is instinctive or needs to be taught and developed by giving the infant opportunities to play is less easy to answer. Play can be considered as a dormant dimension of the human life which, if it is to be developed to the *full*, needs recognition and stimulation from adults in the young child's immediate environment.

A baby is not born able to play but develops this ability with the love and encouragement of his mother or the nurse if the child is in hospital without his mother as sometimes unfortunately happens. Through the security of his relationship with his mother, the child will explore and investigate around him. His first toy and playmate is his mother who sings lullabies and nursery rhymes. So the child learns to play 'peek-a-boo', to bang his own rattle for pleasure and fun and also for the joy and reward of seeing the encouraging response from his parents.

Existing knowledge also indicates that play is important to the child's mental health. Erikson writes 'to play out is the most natural auto-therapeutic measure childhood affords. Whatever other roles play may have in the child's development ... the child uses it to make up for defeats, sufferings and frustrations'. Thus play links the reality of life to the child's fantasies and fears. Young children are dominated by their fears and feelings, but through play learn how to express and cope with these feelings in an acceptable way and in so doing move towards psychologically more mature behaviour. This 'playing out' process often takes the form of reconstruction of painful experiences in order that they can be assimilated into the child's experience. Piaget suggests in *Play, Dreams and Imitation in Childhood* that the cathartic nature of the play provides the child with a

6

unique individual experience and language to express his subjective feelings, so laying the foundations of normal healthy emotional development.

Freud suggested that the basic need of all human beings is for the instincts to be satisfied; tension results if this need is not met. In play, Freud suggested that children need to go on repeating their play activities until they are able to accept and incorporate a particular experience or experiences. The child therefore uses play as a means to release tensions by reliving experiences in the imagination.

Susan Isaacs, an educationalist and psychologist, based much of her work on observations of a group of schoolchildren with above-average intelligence, but who were in some cases considered 'difficult'. Isaacs is careful to stress that several different kinds of play may be going on at the same time, but that there does seem to be a forward progression in play. One stage follows another. It is important for nurses, teachers and parents to realize that there are these different stages of play and to provide appropriate materials and opportunities for each successive stage.

Isaacs calls play 'Nature's means of individual education. Play is indeed a child's work, and the means whereby he grows and develops.' Play as work may be a difficult concept for some adults to accept. This does not mean that play is unenjoyable, as even when not actually accompanied by obvious mirth and enjoyment, it is highly prized by the player.

Whatever the observations and theories put forward by psychologists and researchers over the past century, all researchers have recognized and stressed the importance of play to children of all abilities, intelligences and cultures. Arnold Gesell considers that even children with above-average intelligence are likely to conform to their chronological age in play. He also warns of the problems for children living in high-rise flats who spend many hours passively watching television, and are denied the time and space for free spontaneous play which is essential to the child's development.

TYPES OF PLAY

Play is rich in its diversity and can take many forms. Often one type will overlap with another. Play can be quiet, or noisy and rough. Play

7

can be exploratory or problem-solving, may involve one player or several. Play can be creative and imaginative for children of all ages. But with each variety of play the child will develop particular skills; for example, creative 'pretend' play enables the young child to develop thought, language and mental ability. Each type of play should at some stage form a part of every child's play opportunities according to his mood, environment and ability. The types of play may be summarized as follows:

1. Exploratory play
2. Energetic play
3. Skilful play
4. Social play
5. Creative play
6. Problem-solving play
7. Hobbies and various leisure-time pursuits (for adolescents and adults)

STAGES OF PLAY

Just as the types of play may overlap to some extent, so too may the stages of play. These are related to the child's age, development and ability, and may incorporate one or more types of play.

It should be remembered that during the stress of illness and hospitalization the child may regress, showing play behaviour of an earlier stage which his mother had previously considered he had outgrown. In just the same way the young child may revert to using a 'dummy' or comforter.

Solitary Play

Babies and very young children about the age of 18 months to two years play very much of the time alone. They like to have mother nearby, but are otherwise unconcerned with other adults or children. The child shows intense interest for very short spans of time but

Solitary play: the child is happily absorbed in his activity.

uses a surprising variety of activity as he feels, tastes, piles up and pulls down the play materials provided. Repetition becomes important. All mothers and sick children's nurses will be familiar with the 'throwing teddy out' game, when the child does this again, again, and yet again, a playful exchange between adult and child.

Parallel Play

In the next stage the child enjoys playing alongside other children with whom he will interact very briefly, perhaps to show something, but basically he continues to play quite independently.

Social Play

A year or so later, between the ages of three and four, the child begins to play with others, usually in pairs or small groups of three or four. The child is learning to share and join in group activities. As the child grows older he uses all stages of play but in a more mature form. Repetition becomes less important and interaction occurs with bigger groups.

PLAY WITHOUT TOYS

Children can play without the use of toys or even the active interest of an adult. Many observations have been documented of children playing in city streets, country lanes and open spaces, creating their own games, often with a quite complex set of rules and structure. Iona and Peter Opie have shown in their book *The Lore and Language of School Children* how common these games are, often noting the same basic game in different parts of the United Kingdom, although coloured with regional variations.

Numerous examples have been recorded in literature, especially in biographies and autobiographies, of children's play without toys. Many of these authors show great perception and insight into the ways and play of children, not only from varying periods of history but also from differing family backgrounds and cultures. Their experiences clearly show the need for children to play whatever their circumstances, in order that they can come to terms with their apprehensions and accept the adult world.

Social play in the out-patient's department: the tea party.

Some of these authors were rather solitary imaginative children who peopled their own world with imaginary comparisons or sought particular comfort and friendship in their pets, soft toys or dolls, with whom they shared their sorrows and their joys. The poet John Betjeman writes in his poem 'Summoned by Bells':

> I heard the church bells hollowing out the sky
> Deep beyond deep, like never ending stars,
> And turned to Archibald, my safe old bear,
> Whose wooden eyes looked sad or glad at me,
> Whose ample forehead I could wet with tears,
> Whose half-moon ears received my confidence,
> Who made me laugh, who never let me down,
> I used to wait for hours to see him move,
> Convinced that he could breathe.

11

This word song graphically illustrates the fears and feelings of one small boy but they can be mirrored by many other quiet, solitary creative children from all walks of life.

Ward Games without Toys

Play without toys may also occur in hospital, but because of the nature of the environment and the effects of hospitalization this type of play tends to be limited and restrictive. David Hall in *Social Relations and Innovation: Changing the State of Play in Hospitals* recorded examples of hospital games in children's wards. To give one example, he writes: 'Another game that was invented in the ward to suit the situation was one that expressed children's feelings about the cleaners. Children in bed soaked paper tissues in water from their jugs and hurled the tissues at a globe lampshade hanging from the ceiling. Successful shots stuck to the lampshade, and this the children said represented the head of the chief ward domestic. The game was played in the evening, and at the morning cleaning of the ward, the evidence was still there for everyone to see'. The challenging of ward authority acted as a bond for the children who participated in these games, which created some problems and conflict for the ward staff.

If organized play and toys are unavailable children will become bored and frustrated, resorting to occupying themselves with whatever comes to hand in the ward. The quieter child may become increasingly apathetic and withdrawn in this situation. As the hospital ward does not provide a very creative environment for unsupported play the child may resort to playing with such unsuitable, and even dangerous, objects as water taps, electric light switches and plugs, wound dressings, bandages, tubes and plasters, and buttons, press studs or hooks on clothing. He may also play with his own body or fight with other children, both unsatisfactory activities.

DESTRUCTION IN PLAY

There is a tendency to regard children's play as always being joyful and constructive, but for some children destructive play is a stage of development which must take place before constructive play can begin. Observation of children's play shows that destructiveness in play can take many forms such as breaking toys or knocking over other children's games, and this may be frequently repeated.

Aggression is present in all of us. It is therefore normal and natural that it should also be present in young children. Aggressive play needs to be recognized and channelled into more socially acceptable forms of behaviour. Sand, clay and play dough which can be banged and squeezed are particularly valuable in this respect, and can be very satisfying as an outlet for tension and anxiety, especially for the child confined to bed or cot.

The nurse needs to understand why a child is being destructive, and be able to accept this behaviour without appearing to encourage it, or to reinforce the behaviour with ridicule. Sometimes the nurse need say nothing at all to the child, but can direct him from his destructive behaviour simply by offering him another play activity which she then participates in with him.

More important perhaps is that the nurse needs to recognize the value of destructive play to the child. Tension that has been building up is suddenly vented in action, with a feeling of satisfaction arising from the destruction. For the adult to treat this action by punishment only serves to reinforce the child's feeling of satisfaction. Such satisfaction is short-lived, and the action will be repeated in order to recapture the satisfying feeling and the full attention of the adult observer.

The aim of the nurse should be to replace the satisfaction derived from destruction with the more lasting satisfaction of constructive play. Children who are not made to feel guilty about their destructive feelings will readily move on to constructive play. The nurse should provide opportunities for creative outlets in painting, modelling, and so on, which will give the children a feeling of great achievement, a means of expressing themselves and of being original. The nurse should remember to encourage and praise the child, either directly by speaking to the child, or indirectly by placing the child's work with his name on the ward shelf, wall or notice board for all to see. If this is done, the child can then point out his own work to his parents or other visitors when they come and also to other members of the staff.

2. The Nurse and Play

The child who cannot play is as severely threatened as the child who is deprived of nourishment.

W. D. Wall

Many health authorities now recognize the importance of play in the care of children in hospital and employ play staff. But just as play is integral to the life of the child, so it should form a positive part of the sick children's nurse's care of the child and his family. The contribution of the play worker to the life of a children's ward can be considerable. However, it remains for the nurse to provide play opportunities for the sick child in the evenings and at week-ends, and during the night should the child become anxious and wakeful. It is important therefore that she understands the importance of play and accepts her responsibility to provide play.

Play in hospital has a special significance and remains the one normal element of life in a strange environment away from home. Nurses also have an important role in encouraging parents to join in play activities. Parents who are resident with their child will often be able to recognize their child's need for play, but it is usually left to the nurse to provide the facilities and the tools to make this possible.

Evaluation of the child's play can be an important nursing diagnostic tool. Through play the child often shows to a sensitive and aware nursing staff areas of patient care that can be improved or modified to meet his needs more appropriately.

NURSING CARE/PLAY EVALUATIONS

Mandy aged six years had been admitted to the ward with a severe attack of asthma. Her mother was not resident but visited daily with

Mandy's younger sister. Soon after admission Mandy, dressed in a nurse's cap and apron, was overheard by a student nurse to say whilst giving her doll an injection in its hand: 'it doesn't hurt but it does'.

This remark was reported at the ward nursing team's daily report session and led to considerable discussion amongst the nurses about what the children were being told when being given injections, finger pricks and intravenous infusions. Although it was the ward policy that the truth should always be told in a positive and supportive manner, from Mandy's account this would seem not always to have happened. It is sometimes easier for the adult in a painful situation to take a 'short cut' and avoid the truth. Discussions were also held with the laboratory technicians and the medical staff, which led to a reduction in the number of injections being prescribed and a set routine being established with the laboratory staff, which involved the child's parent or nurse being present whenever blood was taken.

A second situation which influenced nursing and medical practice in one children's ward occurred when three young children were playing 'hospital' in the ward play room. Sister was sitting in the room with another child and overheard the other children's play, which included a doctor's round. After a while the children, dressed up in their pretend roles, showed professional disagreement which led to the 'patient' being told to stay for ever in hospital.

This encouraged the ward sister to review the ward routine and, after discussion with the paediatricians, it was decided to abandon the traditional practice of the ward round going from bed to bed or cot, in favour of a discussion in the ward office where the caring team could sit down and the ward life could go on uninterrupted. Whenever a child needed to be examined this was done wherever the child happened to be, accompanied by his parents or his nurse.

MAKING PROVISION FOR PLAY

The activity of play provides a means of interaction with peers and staff with whom the children can identify in a lively, positive way. Many children's nurses have observed children moving again, despite pain and discomfort, whilst playing post-operatively, or even following severe burns. Play here has the double advantage of encouraging mobility and minimizing secondary complications and thereby, the length of in-patient stay, as well as providing activity suitable for the child's normal healthy emotional growth and development. Playing definitely seems to spur recovery and helps to alleviate homesickness, fear and anxiety.

The common reason given for nurses being unable to provide play is that 'they are too busy', but this is often a rationalization. It is for the qualified nurse to assess nursing care priorities, to examine and evaluate ward routines. Unfortunately organized play is not always given a sufficiently high priority in the child's total care, with the result that insufficient time is allocated to its provision in the nursing care plan. In order to provide time, routines need to be simplified and inessentials discarded. Questions need to be asked constantly in preparing the child's nursing care plan; for example, does this child need the traditional 4-hourly recording of temperature, pulse and respiration, or the daily fluid intake and output measured? Also what play facilities and activities need to be provided appropriate to this child's present condition, development and need? Just as the nurse would not starve a child because she understands the value of balanced nutrition to growth and development as well as the social and aesthetic aspects of food for health, so she needs constantly to remember that play is integral to a child's social, psychological and emotional development. This is particularly important for the child in hospital who feels vulnerable and isolated away from his normal environment. He also particularly needs the opportunity of play in order to integrate and accept the experience of hospitalization.

If nurses fail to recognize this responsibility for providing play in their total care of the child, they will find their role as sick children's nurses eroded. Their duties and contribution to the health of sick children will become relegated almost entirely to providing clinical care.

HOSPITAL PLAY SCHEMES

In 1963, 'Save the Children Fund' was asked to organize a play scheme at the Brook Hospital, London. As a result of its success, several more schemes were started in other hospitals which admitted children. This work was also supported and encouraged by the National Association for the Welfare of Children in Hospital (NAWCH) and the Pre-School Playgroups Association (PPA). The

16

The nurse makes time to help her patient with his painting.

National Association of Hospital Play Schemes (NAHPS) was formed in 1976 to promote trained play staff to become recognized and valued members of the ward team. Full membership is reserved for practising play staff.

In 1972 the Department of Health and Social Security (DHSS) set up an Expert Group on Play for Children in Hospital in response to the hospital authorities' request for guidance. The report of this group recommended that health authorities responsible for hospitals which admit children as patients should recognize their basic need for play and should meet this need.

Following publication of the Report in 1976 (DHSS: HC(76)5) the DHSS stated that the way ahead lay chiefly in the greater involvement of nursing staff (including nursery nurses); that it was desirable for each hospital with facilities for children to designate a senior member of the nursing staff to have general oversight of the nursing contribution to play, collaborating as necessary with other staff involved, for example, teachers and voluntary services organizers. It was also suggested that if play in hospital was to be expanded more volunteer helpers should be recruited.

Hospital Play Workers

Hospital play workers come from a wide variety of trainings and professional backgrounds. Often they are nursery nurses, nurses or primary school teachers or sometimes residential child care workers. They may take one of the established part-time courses in hospital play at colleges of further education.

The play worker should be considered as a member of the ward team working closely with the sister and nursing staff. It will be helpful if the play worker can attend the daily ward reporting session in order that she is fully informed as to the children's condition and progress. The play worker will also find it helpful to read the nurse's child assignment record taken on admission for all new patients (see pages 42–3).

On appointment the play worker should be given an orientation course to meet hospital personnel working in other departments with whom she will come into contact during the course of her duties. If it is a first appointment in hospital for the play worker she should also be given the opportunity if possible to work alongside another play worker elsewhere in the health district for a few days.

Volunteers for Play in Hospital

Volunteers for play with children in hospital can help provide the comforting and homely atmosphere which is so vital in hospital to fostering and encouraging the child to play. Their contribution is

---

A play worker busy with her charges.

invaluable and should be encouraged, using the resources of the voluntary services organizer and the local community.

'Guidelines' for play volunteers working with children in acute hospital wards have been produced by The Play in Hospital Liaison Committee. These emphasize some of the most important points to understand and accept when working with children in hospital. Each new volunteer for play should be given a copy (see Appendix 2, p. 117).

Volunteers need to be carefully selected, in consultation with the ward staff, by the voluntary services organizer and they remain her responsibility. However, they will need continuing direction and support from the ward sister and nursing staff if they are to obtain satisfaction from their contribution to ward play. Some volunteers will have special talents and skills, for example, a pianist or guitarist can run a music session or a handyman will be able to repair toys in the ward.

To be effective volunteers need training. Responsibility for this rests with the senior member of the nursing staff who has the overall responsibility for providing play. A suitable training programme for volunteers will obviously depend a great deal on local circumstances, but attention should be paid to the following subjects in any training programme:

1. Orientation to the hospital, departments and children's wards
2. The caring team, its members and their functions
3. Hospital etiquette
4. Need for confidentiality
5. The needs of the child in hospital
6. The role of parents

All volunteers should have the opportunity initially of working alongside a more experienced volunteer.

PLAY AND EDUCATION

It is important that education should be provided for children of school age. As children now stay in hospital for an average of six and a half days, the role of the hospital teacher is less than that of the traditional educator inculcating the 'three Rs' but can be important in acting as the bridge between life at school (which has tremen-

Books provide a link between school and ward.

dous significance to the child at home) and life in the hospital ward. For the longer-staying school-age child, or the child requiring frequent re-admissions, the hospital teacher will be able to provide formal teaching consistent with the education programme being followed at the child's own school. The child's own school will usually cooperate to provide the appropriate books, work and projects so that the child can keep in touch with his normal environment and is able to keep pace with his peers.

As a result of the provisions in the 1944 Education Act, the local education authority appoints teachers to hospitals for the education of school-age children. The extent of the service which these hospital teachers give depends upon the average bed occupancy of school-age children. Some local education authorities provide for patients from the age of two onwards. Some authorities may only appoint teachers on a part-time basis, whilst in hospitals where there is a large child population, a hospital school employing several teachers with its own head teacher may have been established.

The ward staff need to work very closely with the hospital teachers; their respective roles should be seen to be complementary in meeting the child's needs whilst in hospital. The nursing staff should ensure that all school-age children admitted to the ward are notified to the teacher, and should indicate when the child will be well enough to receive some school work. Daily changes in the child's condition or any procedures or treatments to be carried out should also be communicated to the teacher. Before being introduced to any new school-age child admitted to the ward, the teacher should be given the opportunity to read the patient assignment records taken by the nurse on admission (see page 42). These will give a first indication to the teacher of the child's abilities and interests.

PARENTS AND PLAY

The role of parents in play is often taken for granted in the home. A common attitude is that Mum and Dad only provide the toys. Obviously the parent does have the role of provider of toys for the child, but parents should also be encouraged to take an active interest in their child's play and its development, and also to be able to express interest and give support and encouragement when needed to their child.

When the child is in hospital the parents, because of their own feelings and concern, may not at first be able to share in their child's play. This is sometimes due to embarrassment or a fear of ridicule if they are seen by other people and hospital staff looking a little foolish, or may even be due to their inhibition at expressing themselves in the hospital environment.

_____

Parents can make a valuable contribution to ward activities and play.

Parents need to be encouraged to join in the ward activities, and to contribute ideas and suggestions. The children will appreciate this involvement of the parents because it helps to bring a more home-like atmosphere into the ward. Parents can make a great contribution to ward activities and play, not only with new ideas and skills but also in providing materials for the making of junk toys (see page 60).

Sometimes parents will need advice about toys and what to buy for their child. Often when a child is admitted, especially as an emergency, the parents or grandparents will turn up with an entirely inappropriate and often expensive toy or game. Alternatively parents may arrive at the ward with a toy which their child is unable to play with at first because of the physical restrictions or limitations imposed by his condition or necessitated by the nursing care. One example of this is that children nursed in plastic isolators (see page 99) must have all their toys sterilized. To produce a much-wanted doll or game which is going to take up to two weeks before it is sterilized (sending the item off for gamma irradiation) and can be played with, will produce great disappointment for the child as well as for the giver.

Whenever a parent brings in a child's favourite toy, the nurse should take care that it is not lost or misused. It is sometimes a good idea to suggest that the parent labels the toy to avoid loss. Distress can sometimes be prevented if a toy is sent accidentally to the hospital laundry, as its label will ensure its return to its owner.

3. Historical Back-ground to Play

Toys are the tools of play and are as old as the history of man. Proof to substantiate this statement can be found in many museums as archaeological discoveries throughout the world have revealed evidence of toys made from a wide variety of everyday materials. The design and use of the child's ball, the baby's rattle, the doll or the toy horse have changed very little. Even cave children had balls made from dried fruit or animal bladders which could roll and bounce. Although each generation produces its own contemporary toys as we can see in today's train set and model cars, the old favourites remain.

Evidence of the use of toys and the importance of play in the development of man can also be seen in surviving pictures and literature. Early Egyptian murals show children letting birds fly with lines attached to their legs; similarly a sixteenth century engraving by the artist Jacob van der Heyden shows a young boy flying a bird in much the same manner. Bestelmeirer, a Nuremberg merchant in the seventeenth century, published what was probably the first toy catalogue.

The common theme of all the evidence available is that toys act as a reflection of adult life and as a bridge from one world to another. It is as though the child is being prepared through play with the necessary skills for the reality of living in the adult world. Toys of the past also provide an illuminating historical picture of the current social life and economic climate. This can clearly be seen in the development of the doll's house. In the sixteenth and seventeenth centuries the possession of a doll's house, or as it was then known, a baby house, was a fashionable status symbol for the wealthy. Doll's houses were also shown to children as a social lesson, in order to form good taste and to teach the girls the domestic arts of household management. Although these carefully detailed and beautifully thought-out houses had limited play value as we would regard it today, they must be classed as toys. One of the oldest surviving baby houses in England, at Norwich, is known to have been given by Queen Anne to her god-daughter. In 1801, Maria Edgeworth wrote in *Practical Education*: 'an unfinished baby house might be a good toy, as it would employ little carpenters and seamstresses to fit it up'.

Toys were not confined to the children of the wealthy; there are many examples of how the children of the poor used their creative skills to convert everyday objects into the desired plaything. The poorest Victorian child could enjoy the popular pastime of bowling a hoop in the street or park by simply using the outer rim of a discarded barrel with a piece of wood. A wooden spoon wrapped in cloth or flannel would become a doll, or even an old shoe with a face drawn on the heel.

In the historical study of toys again and again the same basic toy arises throughout the centuries, amongst many races of differing cultures scattered all over the world. The rattle has been given to babies throughout time, first as gourds with the seeds left inside, later becoming ornate carved objects of silver, ivory or coral, and often endowed with special significance. Some cultures believed that rattles warded off evil spirits from the infant and some considered coral good for the eyes as well as being useful for the child to chew on. Today's nurses would have no difficulty in recognizing these old rattles as the shape has remained virtually unchanged. In modern times the rattle is most usually made of one of the plastic substances and as in ancient times is commonly the child's first toy.

The doll as a toy has a far more complex history in that ancient dolls were sometimes fertility symbols or were held to possess magical properties and were often used in religious rites. In some cultures a representation of the human figure or doll would be placed in a grave to act as a guardian of the deceased. This tradition even existed until the present century when in some communities, if a sailor was lost at sea in storm or battle, a doll representing him

An example of a Victorian educational toy.
(*By courtesy of Constance E. King*)

would be placed either under the doorway of his house or given a ceremonial burial. Dolls created for adult purposes were more likely to survive than the dolls children played with; however, in the British Museum can be seen a rag doll of Roman origin. Fifteenth century clay dolls discovered in Germany were sometimes given to infants at their christening when they often held a coin too as a bonus gift for the child. Dolls were often produced in the seventeenth and eighteenth centuries as fashion mannequins for dressmakers to show their clients. These beautiful dolls sometimes became play-things once the fashion they displayed was outmoded; they are now much sought after by collectors who often have to pay high prices for them in the auction rooms.

Dolls are as popular today as they have ever been, and as in the past, they are made from a wide variety of materials. Modern dolls have a functional quality, often being washable and even designed to drink from a bottle, say Mama, cry and wet their nappies. Modern teenage dolls have large wardrobes and even boyfriends. Boys too now find dolls acceptable in the form of Action Man or the Six Million Dollar Man with bionic parts, dolls that can be endowed with daring and courage.

Antonia Fraser has defined the nature of the toy as being compounded of pleasure, imitation and fantasy. The child's need for a simple toy to stimulate the imagination to play and work through fears and fantasies in order to be able to accept the limitations of the adult world is vital to the child's development. Although there have been changes in manufacturing techniques and child-rearing practices, basically the child's need for toys is as deeply rooted as the play instinct itself and as old as man's history itself.

4. Guide Stones to Play

The first five years of a child's life are probably the most crucial to his future emotional, social and intellectual development. During this period of rapid growth the child lays the foundation of future 'well-being'. Behaviour patterns established in these early years influence later personality development. Play during this important period is essential to personality development, on physical, emotional, intellectual and social levels. In play the child explores his environment, stores his memory and learns to control his feelings whilst learning also the essential skills of everyday living.

The aim of these 'Guide Stones to Play' is to provide the nurse with insight into the behaviour and play of a child in his normal environment at a particular age and stage of physical growth. This compilation is by no means comprehensive, but is intended to serve as a guide or aide-mémoire.

It is important to remember that most stages and milestones during the first five years should be qualified with the words 'usually' or 'about'. Children obviously vary tremendously in their intellectual ability, home environment, position in the family, amount and severity of illness they have experienced, and so on. The ages given serve only as a guide.

Often too there will be considerable overlap between one age and the next. For children (depending to a certain extent upon their previous life experiences) illness and hospitalization involve some degree of regression. This may manifest itself in listlessness, apathy or even hostility, and occur whether the child is nursed in hospital or at home. Mrs Bianca Gordon, psychoanalyst with the Hampstead Child Therapy Clinic and principal psychotherapist with the Greenwich and Bexley Area Health Authority, has drawn the attention of nurses (and other child-caring professions) to the need to understand more about a child's attitude to illness, pain, trauma, dietary control and body restriction. To fully appreciate the needs of an individual child nurses need to know more about the stages of child development to allow them to differentiate between those emotional problems which are appropriate to the age of the particular child and related to his illness and those which are not. It is wise for the nurse or play worker not to expect too much of the child's behaviour and play, but instead to be sensitive to possible regression and make allowances for this by providing suitable toys, play materials and a caring supportive environment.

BIRTH TO 6 MONTHS

From birth to six months is a time of very rapid growth and development which is not confined solely to physical growth.

Physical development. At birth the average newborn infant weighs 3·4 kg; by six months the birth-weight has doubled. The first teeth have then erupted (usually incisors). The hair is growing, and the baby has its own individual and recognizable facial expression.

Coordination of posture and movements. Dominated by primitive instincts at birth, with large uncoordinated jerky movements of the limbs. At six months the baby is able to sit with support, and can hold his head erect. With hands grasped will pull himself up, has pleasure in rocking his own body. Turns immediately to his mother's voice and will show excitement at the sound of

approaching footsteps or simple tunes. Takes everything to his mouth including his feet.

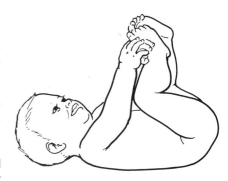

Speech and social behaviour. The infant who initially sleeps 20 to 22 hours out of 24 has become lively and interactive by six months. 'Coos and babbles' to himself and is able to vocalize using single syllables. Laughs at play and will scream with annoyance if frustrated.

30

Play. Loves to watch his mother and listen to her voice. Contact with his mother is the most important aspect of play at this age. Enjoys repetitive games, e.g. 'Hide and Seek' by pulling shawl over the head, also familiar tuneful nursery rhymes, e.g. Pat-a-Cake. Needs very few toys at this stage; suitable ones include rattle, soft ball or stuffed animal, mobile to hang over cot. All should be easy to clean and hand-held toys safe for sucking.

6 TO 12 MONTHS

Six to twelve months is another period of rapid physical, emotional and social growth.

Physical development. Birthweight has trebled by the age of one year. The infant is very active during waking hours but needs something like 12 to 16 hours sleep. Now able to chew well and has between eight and ten teeth.

Coordination of posture and movements. Sits well on his own. Becomes most expert at crawling about rapidly on all fours. Will walk round furniture holding onto the edge with a crab-like action. Still takes objects into his mouth but less often. Can pick up and grip small objects with a fine pincer movement. Uses both hands freely but may already show a preference for one. Drops toys deliberately, and watches them roll away. Learning to coordinate hand and eye movements. Drinks from a cup with little assistance.

Speech and social behaviour. Knows, and immediately turns to, his own name. Babbles incessantly (deaf children do not babble to nearly the same extent as the hearing child) and understands simple commands. With a familiar adult will repeat words and sounds. Demonstrates affection to familiar adults, and clearly differentiates between them and strangers.

Play. Actively seeks the co-operation of his mother or other family member in play. Likes to be constantly within sight or hearing of familiar adult. Toys should be small enough to grasp but not small enough for the child to swallow. Suitable toys include threaded cotton reels or large wooden beads, wooden spoons, sealed cocoa tin of pebbles, washable rubber or plastic animals or dolls, and a saucepan or medium-sized box for filling and emptying.

31

12 TO 24 MONTHS

The infant is very active and curious; his physical growth is less rapid, but he is developing socially and emotionally. Requires constant supervision to protect from danger when exploring his environment.

Physical development. Weighs about 11 to 12 kg and is 76 cm tall. The first set of teeth are almost complete. Crying is now accompanied by tears.

Coordination of posture and movements. By the age of two years has learnt to walk well and may even run. Squats to rest or play on ground. Can throw a ball purposefully and will push or pull trucks or small objects. Can put on some items of clothing, e.g. socks. Able to spoon-feed himself.

Speech and social behaviour. Often about the age of 18 months becomes attached to a soft toy, shawl or blanket whose loss causes great distress. Is outstandingly curious with a vocabulary of about 50 words and will form simple sentences. Talks to himself as he plays. Copies or mimics sounds heard almost constantly. Temper tantrums when frustrated but attention easily distracted. Plays near other children but not with them. No concept of sharing his toys which he will be very possessive about.

Play. Still very dependent on mother or familiar adult. Will follow mother around the home and en-joys copying domestic activities. Able to build a tower of bricks, but drawings and paintings lack any pictorial representation. Sheridan reports that 'girls treat their dolls in a care-giving fashion about 18 to

20 months, boys a little later'. Sheridan and Lowe both report that 'girls show a preference for play with domestic objects and boys for cars or items of transport'. Both increasingly interested in picture books. Suitable toys include wooden bricks, balls, trucks, hammer and pegs, an undressable doll, large cartons for the child to climb in and out of. At this age the child should have his own box or place where his toys can be kept safely.

2 TO 3 YEARS

During this period the development of language is most marked.

Physical development. Growth rate has slowed down considerably.

Coordination of posture and movements. Physically less clumsy. At two and a half years can walk upstairs alone and by three years will be able to go up and down, usually with two feet to a step coming down. Able to ride a tricycle at three years, and clamber over nursery equipment with ease. Fairly skilful at dressing, but needs help with buttons. Dry by day and night.

Speech and social behaviour. Uses an extensive vocabulary of about 1000 words, and asks many questions. Listens eagerly to stories and demands favourites over and over again. Knows several nursery rhymes. In excitement or eagerness stuttering is common. Continues to play alone but alongside other children. Beginning to share toys and sweets with others.

Play. For considerable periods of time creates make-believe play, inventing people and objects, often acting out domestic scenes, e.g. the postman coming. Loves to mimic

adults and help with domestic chores. Able to paint with large brush at easel, pictorial representation emerging. Suitable toys include bricks and boxes, buckets and spades, easy jigsaw puzzles, picture books, imitation household toys, dressing-up clothes. Should be given opportunities to play with water and sand, as well as for energetic activities on climbing frame or swing. A story time should be set aside each day.

3 TO 4 YEARS

Most children aged three to four are ready to profit from, and enjoy, attendance at a nursery school or play group.

Physical development. The child's shape changes from toddler chubbiness to school-age slenderness.

Coordination of posture and movements. Coming up to five years, climbs ladders and trees, runs, pushes, pulls and is able to turn sharp corners whilst running. Expert rider of a tricycle. Manual dexterity well developed. Eats skilfully with spoon and fork. Able to brush teeth and wash face and hands.

Speech and social behaviour. Extending vocabulary and increasing length of sentences. Continues to ask many questions. Able to give full name, home address and age. Listens to and tells long stories, sometimes confusing fact and fantasy. Now plays with other children and understands taking turns. General behaviour self-willed. Sometimes at this age the child invents another self or an imaginary friend whom he talks to and reacts with. May become so real that the 'friend' must be bathed or have a place laid at the table and is frequently blamed for the child's misdemeanours. Will often discard the 'friend' when introduced to other children.

Play. Continues to enjoy building with wooden bricks, but structures are becoming more complex. Play with playdough and real pastry is enjoyed. Percussion and simple wind instruments are popular. Four-year-olds delight in jokes and riddles. More than ever interested in listening to stories. Opportunities for physical exercise and exploration indoors and outdoors should be encouraged. Suitable toys include flat wooden board or easel, paper (newspaper), large brushes and paints, crayons, sand, water, percussion toys, dolls with clothes, toys on wheels, dressing-up clothes, mirror, books.

4 TO 5 YEARS

Ready for school.

Physical development. Taller and much stronger. Able to use sustained effort in activities, e.g. digging or gripping with hands.

Coordination of posture and movements. Active and skilful in climbing, sliding, swinging and jumping. Dances to music with sense of time and tempo. Can now dress and undress alone.

Speech and social behaviour. Speech is fluent, and understanding of abstract words is developing. General behaviour is more sensible and independent. Protective towards younger children and pets. Now chooses own friends. Games are complicated, often with well-defined rules. Developing a sense of time in relation to normal routine for 'today'. Terms like 'the day after tomorrow' are meaningless.

Play. Continues to build constructively with bricks and blocks. Will play spontaneously with friends, even without toys, using rituals and chants of long unwritten tradition, but often coupled with lively contemporary improvisation. Drawings and paintings show well-defined

detail and sense of colour. Make-believe and dressing-up play become more dramatic. Suitable toys include books, toy scissors, paper, beads, thread, painting materials, dressing-up clothes and finery, tricycle.

The author wishes to acknowledge the work of Dr Mary Sheridan.

5. The Child in Hospital

In order to provide play that is purposeful and positive, the nurse needs to give further consideration to the effect of hospitalization on the child and his family.

Admission to hospital can mean a variety of things to different children. Much will depend upon their age, and previous life and family experiences. Another important element is whether the admission results from a sudden illness or accident, or from the hospital's waiting list. Whether mother is able to be resident or not is the most important aspect for the younger child, and even for some older children with special problems such as deafness or visual handicap. Even taking these factors into account, hospitalization for the child means separation from his home, family, friends, school and pets.

The National Child Development Study shows that no less than 43 per cent of the nation's children have been admitted to hospital by the age of seven years (apart from birth). Preparation for this experience is therefore important for all children.

PREPARATION

Ann Hales-Tooke writes in *Children in Hospital: The Parents' View* that 'it is never too early to start talking to small children about hospital, pointing out the big building in the centre of town where the ambulances go. In the same way as one tries to prepare them for other experiences in life, so children should be made aware of hospitals from an early age. Learning about hospital and what happens there can be seen as part of education for life'.

It is always best if preparation for a specific hospital admission is given by the parents, who will be able to relate hospital life to their child's home routine, interests and ability. It should be an honest and realistic picture, but without too much graphic detail and dwelling on the unpleasant aspects. The information should be given in a language and at a pace that the child can absorb. The child should not be told too far ahead of his impending hospital stay. A week ahead is about right for the younger child, but this could be longer for the older child.

Sometimes the parents will ask the nurse's advice whilst attending outpatients, or during a home visit by the health visitor, as to books they can read in preparation both for themselves and for their child. Here is a list of books which parents have found helpful.

Books for Parents

Has your Child been in Hospital? by Joan Woodward. National Association for the Welfare of Children in Hospital, 1978.

Children in Hospital: The Parents' View, by Anne Hales-Tooke. Priory Press, 1973.

Young Children in Hospital, by James Robertson. Tavistock Publications, 1970.

National Association for the Welfare of Children in Hospital: Admission leaflet and comic.

Books for Their Children

Come and See Hospital, by Julie Simpson. Felix Gluck, 1976.

Going Into Hospital, by Althea. Dinosaur Publications, 1974.

Paul in Hospital, by Camilla Jessel. Methuen, 1972.

Mark's Wheelchair Adventures, by Camilla Jessel. Methuen, 1974.

Zozo Goes to Hospital, by M. and H. Rey. Chatto & Windus, 1967.

The Hospital, by F. Peacock. Franklin Watts, 1976.

Thomas Goes to the Doctor, by G. Wolde. Brockhampton Press, 1972 (picture book).

Miffy in Hospital, by Dick Bruna. Methuen, 1976.

Many hospitals and children's departments now produce their own leaflets or comics which can be very helpful to the parents and child. These are usually for children in the older range, five years and upwards, and sometimes include pictures to colour or simple games.

The National Association for the Welfare of Children in Hospital (NAWCH) produces and distributes a range of leaflets and other material which cover various aspects of a child's life in hospital. A publication list is available (see Appendix 1 for address). Nurses too will find this material useful in understanding the wider nature of their work in caring for children in hospital.

All parents need to be aware before admission that their young child may cry when they leave the ward if they are unable to be resident. They also need to understand that many children are unsettled on their return home for a variable period of time. This type of reaction can be expected even from the child who apparently took everything in his stride.

Difficulties for Parents

Some parents find it difficult to prepare their child for hospitalization and this may be due to a variety of reasons. Most often the difficulty relates to their own anxiety about hospitals and medical treatments which results from a bad experience in their own childhood. These parents will need very special help, which is probably best given by the health visitor or the school nurse who may know the family and the child well.

Unfortunately there are still parents who threaten their child with hospital if they are 'naughty', which obviously colours the child's experience and adaptability to ward life. There are also a few parents who deliberately deceive their child about going into hospital, and may even treat the occasion as a pleasurable outing or holiday. Often too, when they leave, the child is told that they are 'just going down the road for some sweets or toys'. The reasons for such behaviour are most complex but these parents really do think that by concealing the truth they are acting in the child's best interests. This sort of situation does pose quite a difficult problem for the nursing staff. The children need the opportunity to talk and express their feelings while at the same time not losing trust in their parents. These parents also need skilled counselling and support from the hospital social worker. Care should be taken by the ward staff not to regard the parents as being difficult or silly.

A three-year-old happily on his way to the radiotherapy department for treatment.

Suggestions to Ease Admission

For those on the waiting list.

1. The ward sister or a staff nurse should attend the outpatient clinics regularly and see all parents and children placed on the admissions waiting list. This gives the child and his parents an opportunity to get to know the nursing staff. Student nurses should also be given the opportunity to attend from the ward.
2. A visit to the ward, accompanied by a member of the nursing team, is arranged. A good time for this is after lunch or late afternoon, when the operating list and treatments, etc. are finished. The visits should be well planned and the mother given the opportunity to meet other parents on the ward and to see the accommodation provided; she should also be given time to ask questions about ward routine, etc.
3. The date for admission should avoid as far as possible any family arrangements such as holidays, birthdays or the arrival of a new baby. The date should be sent in good time. It is also useful to send the hospital admissions leaflet at this time.
4. The health visitor should be informed of impending admissions and liaise with the school health staff if necessary.
5. The hospital social worker should be involved at an early stage, if indicated, to avoid later social problems for the parents, e.g. help with travel arrangements for visiting where the distance is great or if the family has financial problems.
6. The mother should be advised to let the child help pack his belongings and clothes for the hospital stay. It is also quite useful to let the child see the preparations for his return home, e.g. clean clothes ready, etc.
7. It is very important that the child brings with him any prized object, no matter how disreputable his mother may feel it to be outside the home. A new toy is not a substitute. A young child may have a dummy, blanket or pacifier which helps him to sleep. This should always accompany him to hospital and remain within reach during his stay. It may be advisable to put an identification tag on it to prevent accidental loss in the laundry or waste-bin.
8. The mother or father should be advised about 'living in' during the child's admission, and how to make the necessary arrangements.

ADMISSION

For any child admission to hospital can be a bewildering and frightening experience, compounded of noise, strange smells which pervade the wards and long corridors, and the sight of so many people milling about all wearing white clothes or unfamiliar uniforms. All this comes at a time when the sick child has a great need for his own familiar things.

The indignity of being stripped of his own clothes and being given a bath when he had only just had one before leaving home can be distressing and embarrassing to the child who has left the comfort and security of his own home and family. Mother's presence can help a very great deal to alleviate her young child's distress or an older child's apprehension. But the mother needs to share in the management of her child and should be actively involved as far as she is able, according to the rest of her family's needs and her own feelings about hospitals.

Joan Woodward writes in *Has Your Child Been In Hospital?*: 'Most parents have strong fears of being criticised. These are highlighted when a child goes into hospital. A mother has asked me "How can I explain that my child of five still has a dummy; what will they think of her?"' Parents often suffer from feelings of guilt about their child's illness or hospital admission. The nursing staff need to recognize these feelings in order to give the best possible care to the child by responding to the parents in a sincere and helpful way. The parents may feel the need to ask a great number of questions, which may be asked repeatedly of different members of staff. The staff should understand and answer all questions instead of labelling the parents as being difficult or awkward and avoiding them.

On admission, the nurse to whom the child has been assigned should introduce herself by name and take time to complete a questionnaire on the lines of the one below. The nurse should encourage the child as far as possible to answer the questions in his own words. By enlisting his help in this way, the nurse can assess the child's level of comprehension and verbal skills, providing clues and insight on which to build her relationship with the child. If the child is too young or incapable, the mother will appreciate being asked to provide the information which is special and important to the nursing care of her child.

Nursing Admission Questionnaire

Name of patient _____

Age last birthday _____   Birthday _____

By what name is the child known? _____

Names of other children in the family

    Brothers _____   Ages _____

                _____   _____

    Sisters   _____   _____

                _____   _____

By what name does he call his granny? _____

Milestones

Does he sit up without support? _____

Can he feed himself without help? _____

Does he use a spoon, fork or knife? _____

Does he drink from a bottle or cup? _____

Does he go to day nursery/nursery school/play group?

_____

Does he go to day school? _____

Does he go to an ordinary or special school? _____

What is his usual bedtime? _____

Does he sleep alone? in a pram? _____

                      in a cot? _____

                      in a bed? _____

With whom does he share a bed? _____

Does he take a favourite toy, dummy, comforter or 'Bye-Byes'
to bed with him? _____

Has the child brought this article with him? _____

Toilet training

Does he wear a napkin? _____ by day? _____

                                  by night? _____

Are his toilet habits well established? _____

                  still very new? _____

Does he use a pot? _____

What does he say if he wants to pass water? _____

What does he say if he wants to have his bowels open?

_____

Diet

Is his appetite good? _____

Is his appetite capricious? _____

What is his favourite dish? _____

What is his favourite beverage? _____

Occupation

What types of toys does he like best? _____

What are his favourite games? _____

Does he watch television regularly? _____
    What times _____

What is his favourite television programme? _____

Does he belong to Scout/Guides/other outside clubs etc.?
_____

Does he or the family have any pets? _____
    Specify _____

Has he ever been away from home? _____

If under five years, has he ever been separated from his
    mother? _____   State reason _____

Has he ever been to hospital? _____
    State reason _____
    At what age was this? _____

Any special points of interest? _____

What is the child complaining of? _____

Any pains, deformities, etc.? _____

Does he know why he has come to hospital? _____

Does he know how long he is likely to stay? _____

Is mother/father living in with child? _____

Note for the child's own nurse. Admission to hospital and
    separation from the family (and the mother in particular) may
    be a frightening and even harmful experience for young
    children. By knowing as much as possible about your patient
    you can help minimize any emotional trauma and give a
    feeling of security to both child and mother.

When the questionnaire has been completed, the child and his
mother should be shown their beds and lockers as well as the rest of
the ward geography, particularly the playroom, kitchen and
lavatories. Whilst it is desirable to have family grouping in the
children's ward, i.e. children of all ages and both sexes in the ward,

care should be taken as to where a child's bed and belongings are situated. An adolescent patient or a child with headaches will appreciate the quietness of a side room, but a diabetic child of seven years admitted for stabilization will prefer the main ward. Each child should be aware of his own space or territory which is special to him. A pictureboard above his bed will be useful to pin on posters of pop stars, cards or the child's drawings.

Introductions can be made to a few of the other children and parents, but care should be taken at this stage to avoid confusion by too much information.

NURSE–PATIENT ASSIGNMENT

The child should be handled by as few people as practical during his stay in the ward. Each nurse should be allowed to become really familiar with a small number of children and in some instances with an individual child, rather than being allocated to tasks all over the ward. The nurse herself will derive great satisfaction from getting to know a few children and their families well. This is much more important in the care of sick children than nursing specific disease entities.

Off-duty rotas need to be arranged well in advance, in order that continuity can be achieved in the allocation of particular members of the ward nursing team to particular groups of children. This makes it much easier for the child to relate to his own nurses, and enables the nurse to plan daily care on an individual basis according to need. With the mixed grade nursing team usual in most British hospitals, the ward sister will allocate the nurses in training according to experience, under the supervision of specially qualified nursing staff. The Report of the Committee on Child Health Services (1977) recommended that there should be an increase of Registered Sick Children's Nurses for children's wards and departments.

In some cases it is quite impossible for the mother to be with her sick child. It is then important to give the child a 'mother substitute' in the person of a nurse, play leader or other member of the ward team who can give a reasonable degree of continuity of care. The child who is faced with a variety of nurses will feel lost and bewildered, a situation which may well result in serious consequences to his emotional well-being and development. To give the child a mother substitute (and this must be the same person for the majority of time during the child's stay if she is to be effective) is particularly important for long-stay children, young children and those with specific handicaps, e.g. impaired sight or hearing, or troubled backgrounds. The experienced children's ward sister will know how best to allocate her staff according to each individual child's needs and the ward priorities.

THE STAY IN HOSPITAL

With the cooperation and help of parents and other members of the ward team, the aim of the ward routine should be to achieve as normal an environment as possible. Flexibility should be the keynote. Obviously emergencies will occur and operating times have to be scheduled, but the day-to-day care should not be fixed to a rigid timetable. This will allow for the continuation of normal childhood activities, both for play and education. Children in hospital for long periods also need opportunities for outdoor activities if their condition permits and, if possible, weekends at home. A flexible ward routine should allow for this.

Food is of great importance to those in hospital and especially to children. A choice should be available and individual tastes catered for. Mothers will appreciate the opportunity to bring in a favourite dish or beverage for their child. This is particularly important to families of ethnic minorities who, even though they may have resided in Britain for several years, often retain traditional eating habits. The child's medical condition and any special diet ordered as part of his treatment must always be taken into account when food is being brought in from the child's home.

Using a bedpan or urinal may be a very worrying experience for a child who at home is used to going to the lavatory. Occasionally a previously dry child will start to wet the bed again or will have an 'accident' after unsuccessfully sitting on a 'pot'. This is part of the regressive behaviour so often seen when children (and even adults) are admitted to hospital. The nurse should take great care to reassure the child and the parents that this is a temporary situation which will pass. On no account should the nurse indicate by tone of voice or attitude any displeasure, as the child himself will often be distressed at his incontinence and needs understanding.

6. Play and the Sick Child

It is hoped that this chapter will act as a 'springboard' for nurses and others involved in providing opportunities for sick children to play in hospital and at home. The ideas included are by no means comprehensive but should be seen as a guide, or as a base on which to build and extend the original activity. There are many books now available that give more detail for craft activities; a list is given in Appendix 1.

PAINTING

We all derive great pleasure from the colours we see and enjoy using them in our choice of clothes and home decorations. Children too need the opportunity of experimenting and using colour from an early age. One obvious way to do this is with painting, a form of self-expression which gives great enjoyment to children of all ages and can be an absorbing pastime. Children respond as individuals to their surroundings and therefore they paint in an individual way. No two paintings are alike and each child has the joy of creating something unique.

Finished paintings can be used, with the child's agreement, to decorate the walls of the Ward and Children's Out-patients. To avoid damage to the paintwork, a rubber adhesive such a 'Blu Tack' can be used; this has the advantage of being re-usable. Care should be taken not to hang the pictures too high for the children to see them easily.

Children in the ward should be able to paint whenever they wish. Younger children may need some direction and it is probably best for them to start with the primary colours (red, blue, yellow) only. All the children should wear overalls, and for the child confined to bed the covers will need protection. When the painting is finished, ensure that the child's name is written on it for easy identification later. The paintings can then be hung up to dry or left flat.

Materials required:
Easels or a good steady flat surface
Non-toxic powder or poster paints
Brushes (about 30 cm long in a range of sizes)
Jars, or non-spill paint pots (e.g. those produced by James Galt Ltd.)
Protective overalls for the children
Plastic sheeting for the beds

Finger/Hand Painting

Edible water-soluble paints are available for finger painting but are fairly expensive. One cheaper alternative is to make a fairly stiff paste with flour or cornflour and water. Divide the mixture into two pots, adding a different coloured paint to each. These thick paints can then be used on a large flat surface, e.g. table or tray.

Another alternative is to use household starch. Make a smooth paste with four tablespoons of starch and a little cold water. Add about 18 oz (just under a pint) of boiling water to the paste, stirring all the time. Boil the mixture until clear and then allow to cool. Divide into several pots and add a different coloured powder paint to each pot.

A third recipe for making finger paints requires the use of food colourants which may be obtainable from the kitchen stores.

Beat together 4 oz of instant cold water starch, 4 oz of soap flakes and 7 oz water, and continue mixing until the consistency of mashed potatoes is reached. Add food colouring to required shade.

Allow each child to select his own colours and put them on the paper or flat surface as he chooses. Placing both hands in the paint, the child then proceeds to work the colours into each other. This activity is particularly suitable for the younger child.

A group of children can make a hand or footprint painting together. Each child's name can be placed under his own print. A range of colours can be used. This can be a useful group activity for children of mixed ages admitted together, perhaps prior to surgery. It is great fun and helps children to interact with one another fairly quickly.

Blot Painting

Fold a piece of paper in half and then unfold it. Place small spoonfuls of finger paints or thick poster paints on the paper, and fold again along the previous fold-line. Very gently rub the paper, squeezing paint between the two layers of paper.

This simple activity never fails to produce lively bright patterns with a delightful element of surprise in the result.

Potato Printing

Materials required:
   Potatoes
   Damp sponge pads
   Powder paints
   Paper
   Flat surface

A potato is cut in half and a simple relief design is made by removing pieces on the cut surface using a knife or apple corer. The paint can be transferred from the prepared potato onto the paper to the child's own design and colour combination. A carrot can also be used for printing; some children may find these easier to hold.

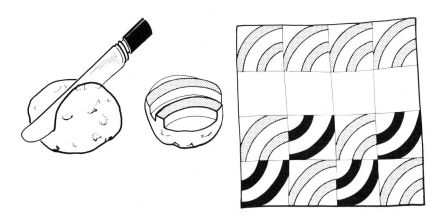

An alternative method is to fold the paper before printing into squares of approximately two inches, and print the potato design in each square.

Older children can carry this activity further by experimenting with other suitable materials for printing, e.g. corks, lino squares and sponges.

PUPPETS

Puppets are a means of self-expression, through which the child can act out the emotions of the moment. A puppet can take on a life of its own and can be very comforting to the child who is feeling isolated and alone. Playing with a puppet can provide a child with a means of communication and of expressing himself to others.

Finger Puppets

The simplest form of puppet, easily and quickly made, is the finger puppet.

Draw faces on the tips of the first and second fingers. Make one face happy, the other gloomy, by simply turning the mouth up or down. A thimble can act as a hat for one, and a small square of paper with a split in it can provide a sombrero for the other. The hand can then be placed behind a bed-table or bedside locker, with the fingers above for puppetry to commence. A conversation can be held between 'Mr Glum' and 'Master Happy' according to the needs of the child.

Alternatively, birds can be represented by drawing a simple beak and eyes on each fingertip. A thin strip of paper can be moistened and stuck round the terminal phalanx of the finger to act as a feather ruff for playing the following game:

Two little dicky-birds sitting on a wall,
One named Peter (show one finger puppet),
 the other named Paul (show the other one).
Fly away Peter (put the first finger puppet beneath the bed
 table or locker edge),
Fly away Paul (put the second one away).
Come back Peter (bring the first finger puppet out again),
Come back Paul (bring the second finger puppet out again).

Many other rhymes can be used with suitable faces on the fingers, e.g. 'To Market, to Market to Buy a Fat Pig'.

50

Paper Bag Puppets

Place a large, clean but discarded CSSD (Central Sterile Supply Department) paper bag over the child's head. Decide on the positions for the eyes and mouth. Take the bag off, then cut the eyeholes and mouth slit in the marked places. (An older child may be able to do this himself.) Let the child decide on the character of his bag puppet and decorate it with paint, scraps of material, etc. The child can then wear the bag and act the part of his chosen character.

A ward play can be produced with the children making their own characters in a story for acting.

Smaller bags to fit over a child's hand can also be used. Another version is to make a bag puppet to fit over the foot of a child whose leg is in traction or in a plaster of Paris splint. This not only provides some fun for the child, but may also be beneficial in encouraging him to use his toes.

N.B. *Always ensure that the children understand that they must never use plastic or polythene bags for paper bag puppets.*

Sock Puppets

Using clean old socks (preferably white) or remnants of Tubgauze or tube netting from the Accident and Emergency Department, place either of these over the child's left hand (or right if the child is left-handed), get him to clench his fist and tuck spare material under the fingers. With a felt pen draw a face on the sock. Encourage the child to speak for his puppet, perhaps even developing a different tone of voice for the character.

Another type of finger puppet can be made using oddments of the smallest size of Tubgauze or tube netting. This can be placed over the finger, then twisted and reversed to fit.

Masks

Give the child a paper plate on which to draw and paint a face. Cut out holes for the eyes and mouth. The face can be decorated with colours, glitter, etc. A fringe of wool can be glued over the forehead. Make small holes at the edge of the plate on a level with the eyes. Tie a length of string through each hole. The mask can then be tied over the ears at the back of the head.

MOBILES

Mobiles are fascinating to watch and fairly easy to make. They are made to be visible, to attract attention as they move with currents of air in the ward. They can be simple or complicated. For the best effect it is important to recognize the relationship between objects, balance, shape and size. A very effective mobile can be made using a theme, e.g. the sky, with shapes cut out of thin card and covered in foil to represent the moon and stars or birds and the sun. Other effective mobiles can be made with decorated paper plates. The themes are endless. Mobiles can be constructed using the basic collage materials (see p. 58), and the frames for hanging can be made from old wire clothes hangers or old wire lampshades.

Materials required will include fine thread for hanging the mobile when finished and also for attaching the items to be hung to either the coat hanger or the lampshade. Noise-makers can also be introduced into mobiles to give variety, e.g. a string of milk-bottle tops

loosely threaded together or streamers made of discarded X-ray film that will shake and rustle in the currents of air.

Mobiles can be made by an individual child or by a group. The children will often get a great deal of pleasure from making mobiles for use in the Special Care Baby Unit or the Intensive Care Ward.

When hanging a mobile above a cot, care should be taken to envisage the effect from where the child lies in order that the child really gets·the full benefit of the mobile's movement and colour; anything that might hang over the child's face should be avoided.

STABILES

Stabiles are free-standing mobiles which can be placed on top of the bedside locker or table. The three-dimensional effect is obtained using bent wire or a coat hanger anchored into a firm weighted

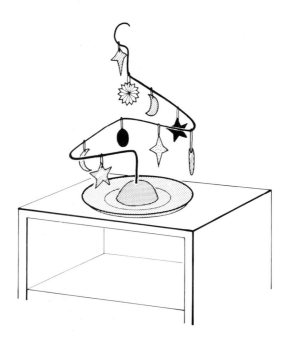

base. The base can be made with clay, Styrofoam (used in flower arranging) or yoghourt containers filled with stones. The wire is held in the stones, then plaster of Paris or Polyfilla, which set quickly, can be poured over. Materials for hanging are the same as for mobiles but the items need to be made on a smaller scale.

'DANGLY' COT TOYS

Toys suspended over the cot can be interesting, attractive and colourful for the child to look at, and he will also be encouraged to touch and feel them; they are ideal for young babies and for the immobile older child confined to a cot. They are easy to make using small toys and also everyday objects that can be hung, e.g. wooden spoons, and empty yoghourt cartons, suspended rather like a bell.

A wooden broomstick is cut to fit the width of the cot. Holes are bored in it at suitable intervals (e.g. four inches apart with a hole half an inch from each end). These end holes are used for tying the rod to

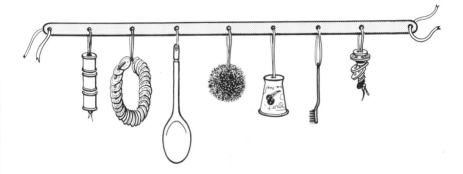

the cot, using tape or string. Tapes attached to the items to be suspended are threaded through the remaining holes.

An alternative hanging frame can be a length of bungee rubber or a luggage grip with hooks at either end (these can be bought at motor or bicycle accessory shops). Care should be taken to measure the width of the cot carefully to ensure that the rubber is neither too taut nor too lax. To give a bouncy feel to one or two of the suspended toys, elastic can be used for hanging.

Remember to vary the toys frequently to give different colours and shapes for the child to see and feel.

PLAY CUSHIONS

Play cushions must be firm, and can be made from foam rubber covered with PVC, or washable cotton or towelling. Cushion toys can be tied to plastic curtain rings which are sewn firmly onto the cushions (about eight to nine for a cushion 12 in. × 12 in.). Tapes can then be sewn onto the back of the cushion for attaching the cushion to the sides of the cot.

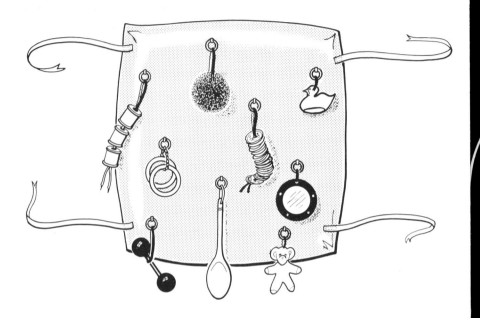

Suggestions for cushion toys. Teething rings, wooden spoons, small soft toys, empty cotton reels, small rubber toys, rattles, soft balls, small mirrors.

MODELLING

Modelling can be intensely satisfying for children of all ages. The child can create, mould and even destroy his creation if he wishes and then start again with the same material. Modelling really does allow the child to 'let off steam' by hitting, squashing and pounding the modelling material again and again. The child confined to bed or wheelchair will find this activity enjoyable and absorbing.

Clay

Self-hardening moist clay has the advantage of hardening within a few days, and once hard can be painted. Although the completed objects do not last in the same way as fired pots, the child does have the satisfaction of creating an object that can be kept and perhaps given to his mother or other family member as a present. Pinch and coiled pots, small animals, slab and moulded dishes as well as abstract designs can be made. Although small quantities of clay in neat polythene buckets are now available in some shops, clay does have the disadvantage of needing to be kept moist otherwise it dries out.

Playdough

Playdough is a good substitute for clay. Commercial playdough is available, but 'home-made' playdough is just as good, and cheaper, and can be made in an even greater variety of colours.

Recipe. Stir together:

2 cups of plain flour
1 cup of salt
1 cup of water with food colouring
2 tablespoons of cooking oil

If the dough becomes sticky, add a little extra flour. Playdough will keep for several weeks and can be re-used many times if it is stored in a plastic bag in a refrigerator.

Alternative recipe

3   teacups of plain flour
$1\frac{1}{2}$ teacups of cooking salt
3   teacups of water
6   teaspoons of cream of tartar
1   teaspoon of liquid paraffin

Mix ingredients in a saucepan over a low heat for about 5 min or so until a suitable consistency is obtained. As the mixture cools, divide and add food colouring. Store in a sealed container or a plastic bag, as this mixture can also be re-used.

Plasticine

Plasticine is a familiar and popular material for modelling and is available in a variety of colours. However, it is too expensive to use in large quantities.

Many items can be modelled with the above materials but they do not have the same lasting properties of items made with clay. However, the child does have the satisfaction of moulding and creating with these materials.

COLLAGE

Collage is a technique used to create a picture, abstract design or decoration for wall hanging, by sticking a selection of materials onto a suitable base. Collage materials can be from items saved and hoarded as well as other odds and ends, e.g. bird feathers found in the garden or dried flowers. Even pasta, dried pulses (beans and peas), pearl barley and rice can be used from the kitchen to make a collage.

Basic equipment. Brushes and adhesive (Copydex, fabric adhesive or wallpaper paste) will be required. Bases must be firm and flat, e.g., thin card, old cardboard cake stands.

A paper collage can be made with different kinds and colours of paper which can be either cut or torn into different shapes. The use of rough and smooth, bright and dull papers, foil, toffee wrappers and Cellophane will all give contrast to the picture. A paper collage is usually most effective when a variety of paper scraps are combined to form an abstract.

Collage can also be used to make calendars or greetings cards. Pieces of paper can be glued onto a base of thin card cut to a suitable size, to make a picture or design. For the calendar, two holes can be punched at the top and string threaded through for hanging, and a small printed calendar can be stuck on the bottom. The child can then write his name on the back, and a greeting to whoever he wishes to give the calendar. For greetings cards, simply fold the card base in half before glueing the final design onto one side. The greetings can then be written inside the fold.

58

Another collage that is more demanding for the older child is to use fabric scraps. Allow the child to choose a piece of material from the rag-bag to cover the base. The child then glues the material to the base and outlines the required picture or design on it with chalk.

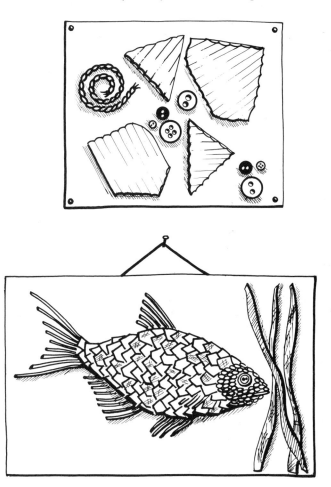

Scraps of material are cut to the appropriate shapes for the picture; these scrap shapes can be moved about to achieve the desired effect before being glued in position. Other items such as sequins, braids or ribbon pieces can then be stuck on to give further effect to the picture.

JUNK TOYS

This section includes some suggestions which it is hoped will stimulate other ideas, for toys children can enjoy making from junk. Junk
includes 'odds and ends' saved by parents and ward staff. It is
important to have a good selection which should include assorted
boxes, cardboard, coloured paper, beads, cotton reels, toilet roll and
kitchen roll cylinders, clean milk bottle tops, etc. (see below). Try
to get into the habit of collecting these things, but they do need to
be stored neatly so as to be easily accessible and identifiable. Old
carrier bags and empty grocery cartons are useful for this storage.

Using Milk Bottle Tops

Plenty of milk bottle tops, stiff card, adhesive and paint will be
needed for making the following toys.

Snake. Thread a needle, tying a large knot at the end of the thread.
Using smoothed-out bottle tops, thread two tops together, with
their edges placed opposite one another, through the middle. Now
thread on all the other tops making sure that they all face the same
way. Fasten off with another knot in the thread, when all the tops
have been used. The more tops there are the longer and slinkier the
snake will be. Cut a narrow piece of felt or fabric and snip one end to

60

make the snake's forked tongue. Stick the tongue onto the head of the snake with some strong adhesive or sew it on with a piece of thread (see illustration on p. 63).

Shields. First cut out the basic shape of the shield in stiff cardboard. Paint the background colour of the shield. When the paint is dry, sketch the design on the shield using a crayon or piece of chalk. Working from the top downwards, cover a small area at a time with strong adhesive and gradually stick the milk bottle tops onto the shield, following the previously outlined design. Elastic or string can be stapled to the sides to act as a harness so that the shield can be worn or hung on a wall.

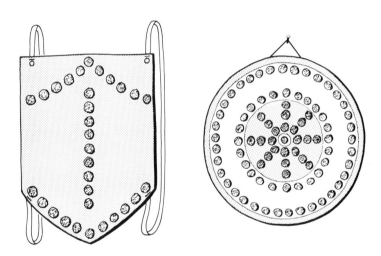

Using Paper Plates

Collect paper plates in various sizes.

An Easter bonnet. Paint the plate. Allow the paint to dry and then bend the front of the plate to give a shape to the head. Decorate with scraps of decorative net, braid, and dried or artificial flowers. Pieces of ribbon, tape or strips of fabric can be stapled to the sides so that the child can tie the hat on.

61

Using Egg Boxes and Shoeboxes

Egg boxes and shoeboxes can be invaluable for making several toys. The cardboard type of egg box is the most useful.

Dalek. Using two shoeboxes glued together as a broad base, glue a further two shoeboxes on top, end to end with each other. Glue egg

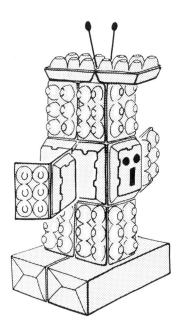

boxes all round this shoebox construction. For the head, use two egg boxes glued together and stuck out at a right angle from the top of the body. Paint with poster paint. Decorate with milk bottle tops and coloured Sellotape. Small lumps of Plasticine on the ends of orange sticks can be stuck in the top of the head to form the antennae.

Cotton Reels

Collect together as many empty cotton reels as you can find. These can be painted in assorted colours, or in some instances left plain. You will also need thin string, buttons, brushes and paints.

62

Cotton reel snake. Using cotton reels which have already been painted in different colours, choose one cotton reel for the head and paint it with two evil-looking eyes which can usually be conveyed quite simply as slits. Tie a large knot in a length of string and thread it through all the cotton reels. Leave two inches of string poking from the head and cut the rest of the string off. Divide the string

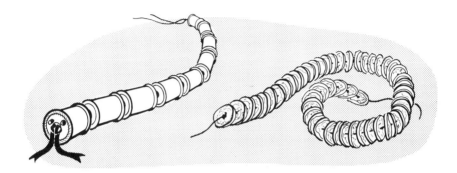

in two by untwisting it. Poke an end through each of the two holes in a button, make two firm knots so that the button is held tightly against the 'head' and the two ends are left hanging out as a tongue.

Reel stringing. Young children of three years and upwards enjoy reel stringing, an occupation which demands a considerable amount of concentration and effort. Provide the child with a long shoelace, with a knot tied at one end, and coloured plastic reels. Alternatively, use wooden reels which have been stained (non-toxic wood stains in a lovely range of colours are made by Dylon) and then finished with a coat of clear polyurethane varnish (non-toxic). The child can wear the completed string of reels as a necklace which is usually proudly displayed to everyone in the ward.

Using Assorted Cardboard Boxes

Boxes of all kinds—round, square, oblong, large and small—will be needed, also stiff card and hardboard if available, and adhesive, scissors and sticky tape. It is also helpful to have a variety of plain or coloured papers, crepe and tissue. Scraps of fabric of all kinds will be useful. Remember also to keep small boxes such as empty matchboxes. Beads, buttons, pulses such as dried beans or rice, will also be useful.

Room interior. Take a box, remove its lid and one side. Paint the inside walls or decorate with wrapping paper. Use a carpet square or remnant for the floor covering. Decide on the room setting; for example, is it going to be a bedroom or a dining room? Use boxes of various sizes, for example, matchboxes or small jewellery boxes, to make the furniture. Scraps of material can be used to make furniture coverings. Inhabitants for the room can be made by dressing peg dolls in scraps of material.

STORY-READING

Story-reading should be an enjoyable time for the reader and for the listeners. All young children love to hear stories, but to read stories successfully is quite an art, for children can become bored and restless. Stories should be chosen carefully, taking into account the child's age and the suitability of the subject matter. If there is time, always read the story yourself first, so that you know what to expect. Make sure that the children are positioned comfortably before you start, and that you, the reader, are too! As you read the children need to be able to see the book the right way up.

Read slowly and with lots of expression, using appropriate animal sounds or differing tones of voice. Try to live the story, but always remember to speak clearly and with understanding. Remember to look at the children often and do not bury your head in the pages of the book. Show the pictures and talk about what is happening on each page. You do not have to keep to the same words, although a child who knows the story may well correct you if you leave out some of the action.

Young children enjoy stories with plenty of repetition, which has a certain magical quality for them, for example *Three Little Pigs*.

One young patient, Andrew, a three-year-old with a malignant disease, insisted on his nurse reading a story to him over the Radiotherapy Department intercom during a course of treatment which was phased over six weeks. It was always the same story, and always to be read in the same way.

Picture books, especially those with pop-up pictures, are very popular with young children, as too are books with pictures on the page facing the story line. Most children enjoy stories about every-day recognizable objects, for example, the teddy with the definite personality, 'Paddington Bear', who likes marmalade.

Young children about the age of two years will only be able to listen to short stories, lasting a few minutes. Older children can listen to stories for up to 10 to 15 minutes and even enjoy a serial reading from one day to the next. Children of all ages like adults to tell stories as well as read them, particularly if the stories are from the adult's own childhood.

Reading Skills

Although children are taught to read at primary school, it is never too early to introduce books to a child. All children should have the opportunity of handling books from an early age and looking at the pictures for themselves.

First steps to reading

Nine months. Enjoys sitting on your knee to look at pictures.

One year. Tries to say a few words after you. Will look through a board or rag book with pictures of animals or simple objects.

Twenty months to two years. Enjoy hearing a story read, will listen for familiar words and repeat these with great glee. Will turn over and look at the pages of a book printed on ordinary paper, but it may be the wrong way up!

Three years. Will handle the book quite skilfully, turning over the pages singly and the right way up. Enjoys looking through picture magazines.

Four years. Likes to tell you a story! Turns over the pages and pre-tends to read. Either knows the story by heart or will make it up for you as he goes along.

Using the Local Library

Visiting the children's library can be an exciting outing for children who are mobile and it is usually possible to arrange for books to be borrowed. For those confined to the ward, an arrangement can be made with the local librarian for a selection of books to be brought to the ward on a regular basis.

MUSIC-MAKING

Children respond to music and sounds of varying kinds by wanting to join in, either by singing, dancing or playing with home-made instruments. Some children's wards have a piano which can be used for accompaniment to songs if there is a member of staff who can act as a pianist. Alternatively the guitar can be used if a member of staff or perhaps a voluntary worker can provide the skill.

There are many books with the necessary words and music (see list below). Alternatively there are long-playing records and cassettes of songs and nursery rhymes. The list below is merely a guide and a full list of the selection of records available can usually be obtained from your local record shop.

Home-made Instruments for Percussion

Drums. Drums are easily made from an upturned saucepan or old biscuit tin. Wooden spoons can be used as drumsticks.

Gong. An old frying pan or saucepan lid which can be suspended will make a good gong. Again a wooden spoon or spatula can be used as the beater.

Cymbals. Two flat lids played together will make good cymbals.

Maracas or rattles. Maracas or rattles are best made in pairs for the children to play. Put some dried macaroni, rice, sand or dried peas in two empty drug tins or liquid detergent bottles. The quality of sound will vary according to the filling. Care should be taken to ensure that the lids of the containers are carefully sealed.

Harmonicas. Hair combs covered with toilet tissue will make a nice brassy sound when held against the mouth for the child to hum against.

Shufflers. Tack or glue sandpaper to one side of each of two wooden blocks (hand-holding size). When these are rubbed together in time, the sandpaper produces a nice shuffling dance-band beat.

Bells. Little bells sewn firmly onto wide elastic to fit around an ankle or wrist are useful to encourage movement and make an interesting sound. An alternative is to sew these bells (obtainable from pet stores or craft shops) onto the child's mittens or gloves.

Useful Song Books

This Little Puffin. Nursery songs and rhymes by E. Matterson. Penguin, 1976.

Nursery Songs and Carols, by F. Walters. Franklin Watts, 1971.

Girls and Boys Come Out to Play, by E. Poston. Bodley Head, 1971.

Faber Book of Children's Songs, by D. Mitchell and R. Bliss. Faber, 1970.

Faber Book of Nursery Songs, by D. Mitchell and C. Blyton. Faber, 1968.

Puffin Song Book, by L. Woodgate. Penguin, 1970.

Singing and Dancing Games for the Very Young, by E. Nelson. Oak Tree Press, 1979.

Best Singing Games for Children of All Ages, by E. S. Bley. Oak Tree Press, 1979.

They Shall Have Music, by Philip Bailey. Oxford University Press, 1973.

Records and Cassettes

Oats, Beans and Barley. An anthology of songs for children. Argo Record Co. Ltd.

Sense and Nonsense. A collection of rhymes and songs. Argo Record Co. Ltd.

What Can I Do? Songs and games to keep children amused. Precision/BBC.

Monday, Tuesday and other children's songs, sung by Mary O'Hara. Emerald.

Oak, Ash and Thorn. Argo Record Co. Ltd.

Older children usually prefer the latest music or songs from the popular music charts. For this information seek the children's advice on what records to borrow from the local library or to buy from record shops.

WATER PLAY

Water is not only a necessary and practical element in our day-to-day lives, but it can also provide comfort and pleasure. Tired persons often find relaxing in a warm bath soaks away tension and worry. Play with water can have the same beneficial effect for young children.

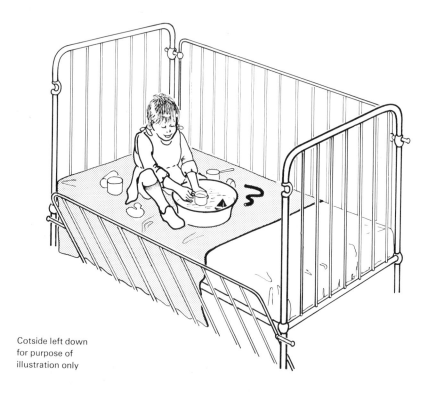

Cotside left down
for purpose of
illustration only

Water for play can be provided in specially designed water troughs, or ordinary plastic bowls and baths may be used. A variety of jugs, syphons, funnels, sponges, corks and piping should be provided for the child to use whilst playing with the water.

For the child confined to bed, protect the bed covers well with plastic sheeting. If there is sufficient space in the cot or on the bed table provide two bowls of water. To provide variation add a small quantity of edible food dye to one of the bowls.

Bubble Blowing

Young children delight in blowing bubbles. Make your own bubble mixture from washing-up liquid and a little water. Add some glycerine or cooking oil (about a teaspoonful to a cup of bubble mixture) so that the bubbles will be stronger and more colourful. A wand to dip in the mixture and shake can be made from a piece of wire or a pipe cleaner. Bend one end into a circle to make a shape like a lollipop. Older children may prefer to blow through a pipe or a piece of clear plastic tubing or a cotton reel.

SAND PLAY

There are some obvious problems for sick children in playing with sand in the ward. Sand is gritty and unfortunately when dry has a tendency to fly about, and get into wounds and under plaster casts. However, there is value in children playing with sand, and ideally there should be a sandpit available in an outside play area (see p. 92). The value of sand as a play material lies in its flexible, versatile nature and in its distinctive texture. Dry sand can be poured and damp sand makes an ideal modelling material; damp sawdust makes a good substitute. Wooden spoons, spades, scoops, plastic buckets and sieves can all be used for playing with sand.

A bed version of sand play can be achieved by using 1 kg (2 lb) of table salt on a tray with a good edge to it.

COOKING ACTIVITIES

Children love to participate in an activity which has an obvious end result that can be shared and enjoyed with others. Cooking will be particularly valued, as parents can be encouraged to join in, providing useful hints and ideas. It will also act as a valued link with the child's own home and family.

Included as part of this activity is the preparation involved, not only in seeing that the appropriate equipment is available (some of which may be borrowed from the kitchen) but also in ensuring that the children's fingernails, hands and wrists are all scrupulously clean before commencing. Table tops should be scrubbed also. Children

69

Pastry-making in progress.

confined to bed will need to be protected with coveralls and plastic sheeting.

Marzipan Sweets

Collect together packets of marzipan (or soya substitute), food colouring, basin and wooden spoon. Divide the marzipan into parts according to the food colours available, and colour, leaving one part plain. Working on a lightly floured surface, the child can roll and press the marzipan into shapes as he wishes, for example, as fruit.

Tarts for Tea

Collect together defrosted packets of shortcrust pastry, baking tray, rolling pin and pastry cutter. Work on a lightly floured table top. Roll the pastry flat. Show the child how to cut shapes and place them in the baking tray. Spoon jam into the tarts and cook in the oven (Mark 5 or 204° C) for 20 min.

Pastry can also be rolled out and shaped into pastry men, decorated with currants for eyes, nose, buttons, etc., then cooked in the oven (Mark 5 or 204° C) for 12 to 20 minutes.

Other Ideas for Cooking Activities

Instant puddings and cake mixes are suitable for the child confined to bed and able to use only one hand for mixing.

GARDENING

Children get great pleasure and satisfaction from observing and taking care of plants. The children's ward, unlike a greenhouse, has its temperature and humidity controlled for the comfort of the children rather than plants. This means that plants in the ward will probably have to put up with a dry atmosphere and often inadequate light. Many house plants need only indirect natural light, so it is only necessary to make the atmosphere moist for them. This can be done by completely enclosing the plants in bottles, covered fish tanks or clear plastic boxes to prevent loss of moisture. Unfortunately, children get bored with plants that need no attention. In a children's ward it is better to plunge plant pots in a trough of moist peat and spray the leaves with a mist bottle every day.

In wards with poor light, grow aspidistra, fatshedera (an evergreen shrub) or *Ficus pumila*, a climber which can be grown as a trailing pot plant or trained upwards against a wall. Some shade-loving bromeliads such as *Vriesea fenestralis* are popular with children because they have central rosettes which can form urns that need filling with water regularly.

Plant Care

Children usually water plants too much or not at all. Deal with this by first grouping plants with similar needs in large trays, but keeping the pots a few inches apart to let air circulate round them. Put simple instructions on the trays, such as 'Water every other day' or

71

'Do not water the cacti until April'. Alternatively circle the appropriate dates for watering on a calendar and place this on or by the plant tray(s).

Plants to Grow

Chinese sprouts. Soak mung beans for at least four hours in cold water. Wash them in fresh water before spreading evenly over a tray covered with damp blotting-paper or flannel. No soil is needed.

Cover with black polythene and put the tray in a warm place. Water the base every day so that it is kept damp, but do not over-water. Sprouts from the bean will be ready in six to eight days. These crisp shoots give a distinctive flavour to mixed vegetable dishes, 'Chinese style'.

Mustard and cress. The seeds of mustard and cress can be sown in the same way as mung beans. Sow the cress three days before the mustard so that the two crops will mature at the same time. Press the seeds lightly onto the moist blotting-paper or flannel, and cover with polythene. When the seeds have germinated remove the polythene. The mustard and cress will be ready 11 to 14 days after sowing. Peas and beans can be grown in the same way.

Citrus pips. Germinate orange, lemon or grapefruit pips in moist peat sealed in a polythene bag. Pot up the seedlings in John Innes Potting Compost No. 2. Keep well watered in a sunny place.

Bulbs. Place spring bulbs, such as hyacinth, on pebbles in a shallow bowl or saucer. Pour water into the container, but do not allow the level to reach the bottom of the bulbs. Keep in the dark until the roots are well formed.

Onion flowers. Put three toothpicks into a large onion and then suspend it over a glass of water so that only the bottom of the onion is in the water. Put it on a sunny window-sill. It will send up graceful green leaves and eventually produce a flower.

Pineapple. Slice off the top two inches of a fresh pineapple and let it dry on a saucer for ten days. Then plant it in a small pot of damp sandy soil. Keep it moist, and in a month, after shoots start sprouting, transplant it to a large pot filled with sandy potting soil. This makes a dramatic and different-looking house plant.

Carrot, parsnip, beetroot and turnip tops. These can all be made to grow more leaves. The cut surface must be kept in a saucer of water and never allowed to dry out. Growth is fairly rapid and the first signs of the new leaves can be expected after a few days.

WARD PETS

The care of pet animals can be of therapeutic benefit to hospitalized children, who often feel caged and vulnerable themselves. As long ago as 1903, studies showed that pets were beneficial to the development of children. More recent studies have shown their value in teaching mentally handicapped children, and many nurses, paediatricians, teachers and social workers will testify to the practical benefits that ensue from encouraging contact between children and pets. Many children's wards and departments now house fish, pet hamsters or caged birds.

Justifiably, considerable concern is expressed over the 'zoonoses', some of which are transmissible from pets to humans, and disease-producing. Other objections levelled against the keeping of ward pets include expense, smell and the amount of time spent on their care.

Whether a pet is kept in the ward or not is a decision that must be taken by senior members of the ward team after considering the effects on the children and staff, and the benefits or possible risks involved.

Suitable Pets for the Children's Ward

Very suitable. Mice, guinea pigs, canaries and other small cage birds, tortoises, cold-water fish, rats, rabbits, clawed toads and invertebrates (stick insects and worms).

Budgerigars are very suitable, but may be a source of psittacosis (organism carried by psittacine birds, e.g. parrots, macaws, etc. may produce pneumonia in humans).

Moderately suitable. Golden hamsters, gerbils, mynahs, frogs, toads and salamanders.

Unsuitable. Terrapins, turtles, snakes, parrots and monkeys.

In the spring tadpoles can be kept for a few weeks but they should be returned to their home pond as soon as they begin to grow legs.

Care of Pets

If a pet is kept, adequate care must be given. Animals are less likely to become ill if they are well managed. One person should be responsible for the daily care of the ward pets and should make appropriate arrangements for their care when she is off duty or away on holiday. Fresh food and water should, as a general rule, be provided daily. Cages must be cleaned and thoroughly disinfected at least once a week.

Animals react badly to sudden changes in diet, temperature or humidity and every effort should be made to avoid these.

A Wormery

Put a few ordinary garden worms in a large screw-top glass jar about two-thirds full of earth. Place a layer of silver sand over the surface of the earth. If the sand and earth are in alternate layers the tracks of the worms will be apparent. On top of this put some dried leaves. Tie a brown paper bag around the jar to darken it. After about a week, you should be able to see the silver sand tracks in the earth where the worms have gone to the surface to drag down the leaves.

WARD NEWSPAPER

Pat Azarnoff writes in *A Paediatric Play Programme* of the value to children, parents and staff of publishing a ward newspaper. This would encourage the children to be involved with one another in a variety of activities, including not only writing and drawing, but also giving interviews, preparing layouts and organizing the distribution of the paper. Obviously the editorial staff will need to be of an age to read and write, but production of a ward newspaper or broadsheet does allow children of all ages to take a more active interest in their environment. The newspaper provides a forum for them to voice their feelings and perhaps to suggest improvements in ward routine and conditions.

The following poem was written by a 12-year-old boy for his hospital teacher and graphically conveys his feelings about his own situation in hospital.

At Hospital

When I first came to hospital
    And wasn't settled in,
I had a thumping headache
    And I couldn't stand the din—
Of the tele and the radio,
    Which when on at full blast,
Tempted me to get better
    And back home extra fast!
(You might like to know,
    I didn't though!)

The food I suppose is really
　　Not all that bad,
There's some though I'd rather
　　Not have had!
The beds are usually far from soft,
　　But I'm growing used to that.
The only thing, you start to miss
　　Your family and your cat!
At first you get confused
　　With all the nurses' faces.
It's nice (but not what you can
　　Really call the best of places!)

Reading children's stories, poems and even jokes about hospital experiences can provide insights for a sensitive ward staff into the behaviour and needs of individual children. The newspaper can provide a salutary learning experience for all staff and may even act as a catalyst to promote change.

To produce a newspaper satisfactorily, there should be facilities for typing and duplicating. Sometimes this help may be available from a ward secretary or voluntary worker who has some basic secretarial skills. This is not always possible. A satisfactory alternative is to produce a single illustrated broadsheet of ward events, stories, poems, jokes, etc. This can be pinned up on a wall or notice board for all children, parents, visitors and the staff to read.

SCRAP-BOOKS

Children of all ages enjoy making scrap-books. They can either be made by one child working alone or by a group of children working together as a team. Scrap-books can be bought ready made, but a cheaper alternative is to make them from scrap paper and cardboard.

First Method

1. Cut fairly stiff cardboard to the required size. Fold in half down the centre, open out flat again and make three holes down the fold line.

2. Cut the scrap paper to the same size as the cover, fold in half, open out flat again and place on the cover.
3. Using a bodkin or darning needle threaded with embroidery cotton or several thicknesses of ordinary sewing cotton, sew in and out of the three holes several times. Finish the thread off in a bow on the outside of the cover.
4. Fold the cover along the previously made line (paper inside). Decorate cover.

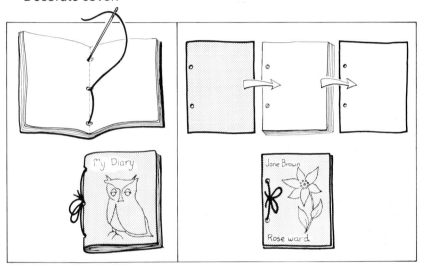

Second Method

For this method you will need a hole puncher.

1. Cut two pieces of cardboard the same size for the cover. Punch two holes in exactly the same places in each piece of cardboard and in the scrap paper which can be in single sheets or folded.
2. Thread ribbon, tape or string through the holes and tie in a bow (rather like a file notebook).
3. Decorate the cover.

The scrap-books can be filled with pictures, photographs, etc. cut out of mail order catalogues, old Christmas cards or magazines. Older children can provide captions, poems or stories about the pictures if they wish to do so. The finished scrap-books wiill give much pleasure to younger children in the ward when they are ready for use, as well as giving pleasure to the children who made them.

HOSPITAL PLAY

Any hospitalized child is faced with a considerable amount of stress, in that he often has to adjust to separation not only from his parents, but from the security of his family life and routine as well. He is also bewildered and confused by the strange environment of the hospital world, an environment which appears hostile and tension-creating at a time when the child may also be feeling ill and vulnerable. Even when the mother is resident with her child and can interpret this environment and provide security for him, the child will often have to experience painful procedures and a restrictive routine. Opportunities must be given in play for the child to communicate his feelings and tensions in order to be able to integrate these experiences.

Following a nursing or medical procedure, e.g. having a throat swab or an intravenous blood sample taken, many sick children's nurses will have observed children repeat or play out the situation. The child will often use his teddy or doll for this or sometimes involve another child in the ward.

Seven-year-old Alice, who was receiving renal dialysis twice weekly, would, whilst in the unit for her treatment, insist on attaching tubes to a mock fistula in her current companion, a 'Winnie-the-Pooh' bear. This was carried out most realistically using a sound technique! 'Winnie' always had at least one bandage or plaster on his arm, and like Alice was submitted to a restricted fluid intake.

Other children sometimes invent animal or doll hospitals; one inventive boy designed a monster haven. Here in play the child can safely learn to master his experience of a painful situation in which he felt like a helpless victim, in an active and positive way and thereby attain control of his feelings of impotence and anxiety whilst in hospital.

A Hospital Corner

An area should be set aside in any ward playroom to serve as a 'hospital corner'. Children who have to undergo painful procedures and operations can be helped if they have suitable play materials, such as discarded hospital items, with which they can recreate situations and experiences and thus come to terms with them.

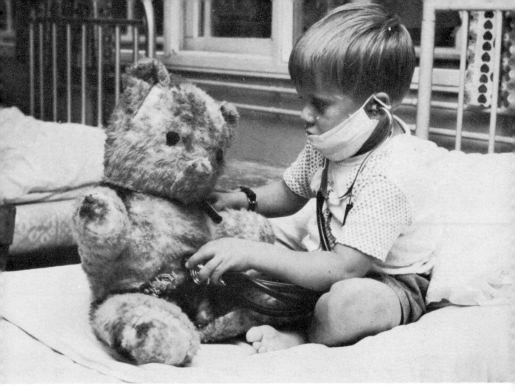

Hospital play helps a child to come to terms with his experiences in hospital; here teddy is the patient.

Basic equipment should include:

Box containing bandages
Empty medicine/tablet containers
Teaspoons
Syringes without needles
Stethoscopes
Anaesthetic face masks
Dressing packs
Disposable gloves
Nurses' caps and aprons
Cot blankets and pillows

A bed can be made by pushing two chairs together, if a small size bed is not available.

Dressing-Up Clothes

Children need a variety of clothes for dressing up. These will either be given by parents or can be obtained, usually quite easily, from jumble sales. Dressing-up clothes need to be washable and should be made from materials that are colourful and of interesting textures; they should be simple for the child to put on and take off.

Dressing-up clothes should be provided for boys as well as girls, to enable the children to dress up as mothers, fathers,nurses, doctors, ballet dancers, postmen, policemen, brides and princesses.

A selection of clothes might include the following:

Long and short dresses of simple design
Long and short skirts
Frilly petticoats
Hats, scarves and gloves
Handbags and shopping baskets
Trousers of assorted sizes
A variety of headwear which could include hair bands, bridal
    coronets and crowns

Other useful properties for dressing up should include old nylon curtains, lengths of material, ribbons, necklaces, sashes, brooches and badges, and even spectacle frames without the lenses.

Doll Play

Dolls provide vehicles for the child to act out hostile feelings safely. They also provide companions for the child to nurse, bathe, feed, punish and talk with. Both boys and girls need to have this opportunity of playing with dolls, to play out their fears in a situation in which they feel insecure.

A variety of dolls will be required, black and white, of differing sizes, both male and female. Dolls that are washable and, if possible, unbreakable should be used. Ideally the dolls should have movable, flexible heads and limbs, and be easy to dress and undress. Suitable clothes both for boys and girls should be provided. These clothes should be washable with easy fastenings. Both day and night clothes will be needed for the dolls.

7. Play Facilities in the Ward

As was discussed in the Introduction, play is the working language of children and forms an integral part of the child's normal development. The value of play during any hospital experience for the child is based not only on this underlying philosophy, but also on the recognition of the various benefits that play can bring to the child (and the staff). The provision of appropriate facilities for play in the ward is therefore important.

PLAY SPACE

The advantages and disadvantages in the use of playrooms are usually related to their proximity to the children's ward. To be really functional a playroom must be in the ward, not outside it. The children, parents and staff must be able to look in and out of the playroom easily without it aesthetically becoming a 'fish bowl'.

One young child, Timmy, aged three years, who had been in hospital for two days refused to go into the playroom which he did not appreciate was part of the ward. It was discovered from talking with Timmy that he feared his mother would not be able to find him when she arrived in the mornings, as he was unable to look out into the ward from the playroom.

Play can take place anywhere in the ward, either at the bedside or around a group of tables and chairs which act as the hub and focus for play for those children who are up and about.

In the United States the hospital playroom is regarded as the child's sanctuary, doctors and nurses in uniform are often excluded and on no account are examinations, treatments, or even recordings

The blackboard is a much-used piece of equipment in the ward playroom.

of blood pressure, temperature, pulse and respiration allowed. This approach is not found in the United Kingdom, where play is regarded as being part of the child's total experience, to be shared in by those involved in his care. In the family situation this would be the child's parents, but in hospitals where total care is the responsibility of the nursing staff they must assume this role.

Children are seen by doctors and nurses in the playroom where quite often minor nursing procedures may be carried out at the discretion of the nursing staff. On these occasions, the presence of other children can be helpful and supportive. However, procedures such as the changing of dressings and removal of tubes are best carried out in the treatment room or at the bedside. This allows the child to cry and voice his distress if he needs to, without fearing ridicule from his peers; equally, this approach avoids the other children seeing a situation which they may identify with and fear because of their shared experience of being in hospital.

Modern hospital designs which include children's wards or departments will provide space for play, usually in the form of a completely separate playroom which is light and spacious with low glass partitions into the ward. It is important for the children in the playroom to be seen and for the children themselves to see into the ward. Where necessary for secrecy (perhaps when the children are preparing decorations for a special event) bright decorative curtains can be drawn across the windows. Wall space with notice boards for pinning up paintings and posters is essential. It is a good idea if hooks can be placed at intervals in the ceiling for hanging mobiles, balloons and other decorations.

A full-size mirror standing on the floor against one wall together with free-standing blackboards will also be useful for the children (alternatively one wall can be painted with special blackboard paint up to a height of about three feet).

The doors of the playroom should be half glass, and wide enough to allow for the entry of a child in a bed. The door should be high enough not to impede the entry of hanging intravenous infusions. The angle of the door into the corridor or ward should not be too acute or difficult to manoeuvre into, as traction or extension apparatus will be attached to some children being moved into the playroom on their beds. Where feasible, French windows which open onto an outdoor play space should be incorporated in the design.

PLAY FURNITURE

Some children will be confined to bed and if their beds cannot be moved into the playroom, play must be taken to them in the ward. A trolley with ridged edges (to prevent toys falling off) which is light and easy to move when stocked with games, books and other items is useful for this.

Other furniture should include tables at child and adult height, chairs in assorted sizes and shapes, and a rocking chair. Children enjoy being rocked, especially if they are unhappy or distressed. A bookstand that can be used to partition off a quiet space or a domestic corner in the playroom is also useful.

Other fittings might include the following:

A hand basin with hot and cold water, and a towel dispenser

A row of hooks for hanging up plastic overalls that are worn by the children during painting or messy play

Open shelving on which can be placed a variety of items

Storage

One of the most important requirements in the provision of play for children in hospital is adequate storage space. A sufficiently large stock and range of games, jigsaws and toys will be needed as well as other essentials such as papers, paints, brushes, crayons, etc., which can all take up a surprising amount of space. A fairly big play stock is required in order to provide for the play needs of a rapidly changing child population of varying ages, abilities and needs in the ward. Storage space will also be required for the creative toy materials (see page 91). If possible a small area should be set aside for toys that are in need of repair and maintenance. 'Safe shelving', away from small prying fingers, will also be required for keeping games still being played or for unfinished handiwork.

Storage space of three kinds will be needed: open, closed, i.e. lockable, and personal.

Open storage. Open storage space can be in the form of shelving and cupboards to which the children, parents and staff all have free access at any time. The items kept here will need frequent review in order to maintain stocks.

Closed storage. A lockable cupboard will be required. This is necessary for the storage of more precious items. Surprise toys and games for special occasions can also be kept here. The key for this cupboard should be in the charge of the ward sister or play worker.

Personal storage. Ideally each child should have his 'special place' for keeping his own toys. Although it is usual to provide each child with a bedside locker, these are really only adequate for clothing and toilet items. Wooden toy lockers on wheels and of a size to fit under a bed or cot can be provided; they can also serve as a seat. These lockers are, however, rather expensive, although a good long-term investment. A cheaper and perfectly adequate substitute is a toy bag. This can easily be made from scraps of material sewn into a bag which will fit over a wire clothes hanger. The bag can then be hung from the child's bedside locker. One advantage of this design is that the bags can easily be sent to the hospital laundry for cleaning.

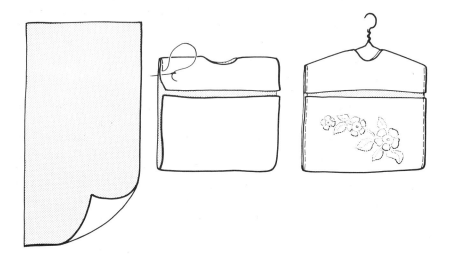

CHOICE OF TOYS

Toys are generally designed with a child's age, sex and particular stage of development in mind. However, toy manufacture can be a profitable business, and some toys are made and packaged to appeal more to the adult buyer than to be of value in a child's play. As good toys are expensive, great care and discrimination should be shown in their purchase, taking particular account of their safety, function, versatility and ease for cleaning, also the average mental and physical development of the children who will be using the toys. Many cheap toys are a waste of money as they tend to be fragile and have a short active life. As with other purchases, it is better in the long term to go for quality rather than quantity.

Accidents with toys are frequently due to their being misused, but there are inherent risks in the use of certain toys, e.g. skateboards or scooters, which must be taken into account when buying the toy or allowing it to be used in the ward. The nurse should always ensure that the child understands how to use the toy safely.

The British Standards Institution have issued a standard for the safety of toys (Safety of toys. BS 5665: Part 1: 1979. EN71: Part 1). This standard applies to toys for children and sets out the requirements and methods of testing for the physical and mechanical properties to be taken account of in the manufacture of toys. The manufacturers who meet the requirements of the standard are allowed to show the kite mark which purchasers should look out for as a sign of quality. The presence of the kite mark, however, does not release parents and nurses from their responsibility for watching the child while he is playing.

Most children's wards are given toys at Christmas, and in some hospitals 'The League of Friends' or other voluntary organizations provide funds for the purchase of toys, games and play materials. It might help to have in readiness a 'shopping list' of supplies, toys, games, etc. so that ideas are forthcoming when funds are offered. Donors often find it more rewarding to give or raise funds for known objectives. Remember that as some toys will be very popular and have considerable use, provision should be made for their maintenance and replacement when necessary. Some funds should be set aside for the purchase of disposables, e.g. paints, paper, crayons, glue, etc.

Accidents During Play

Every precaution should be taken in the ward environment to eliminate hazards and thus avoid accidents. This is particularly important in relation to the regular maintenance and checking of all toys and play equipment that should be carried out as a matter of regular routine. However, accidents do sometimes occur and, no matter how trivial, should always be reported to a senior member of staff.

The health authority is held responsible for the treatment and care of all patients. If a child is injured whilst playing, either in using a piece of equipment or by another child, first aid treatment should be given and a doctor notified. An accident form must be completed without delay and the doctor's signature may be required. Names and addresses of witnesses too may be required. Any item of equipment involved in the accident should be labelled and kept

Bricks and a saddle seat engine make practical hardwearing toys with lasting appeal.

locked, in case it should be required as evidence. Once the matter has been decided, the item may be returned to the play stock, but only after careful checking to ensure that it is not faulty.

It should be remembered that the accident form is a confidential document (reference HN(55) 66).

Toys for Different Age Groups

Babies. Babies need interesting things to watch, sounds to hear and shapes to handle.

1 to 6 months. Mobiles, rattles, soft dolls, teething rings, bells and shakers, floating bath toys, 'pull a tune' boxes.

6 to 12 months. Nesting blocks, brightly coloured stacking cups, activity centre, action ball, wooden fitting toys, mirror.

Toddlers. Toddlers are starting to match, sort and fit objects together, and to understand the concept of size; they are learning to recognize colours.

12 to 18 months. Pull/push toys, cuddly animals and dolls, wooden toys big enough to mount and sit on, stacking toys, posting box.

88

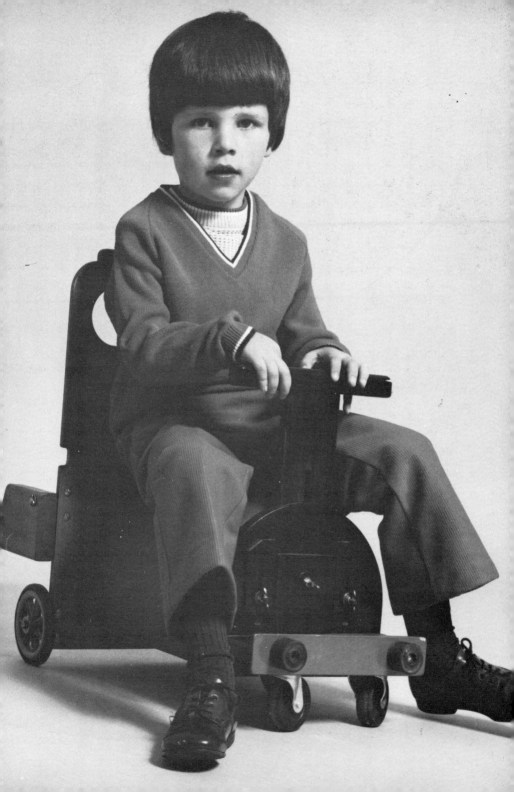

18 months. Hammer and peg toys, wooden animals, sand box, digging equipment, simple wooden jigsaws with lift-out pieces, rag doll, teddy bear, screwing toys.

2 to 2½ years. Make-believe play begins about this age. Doll's equipment and clothes, plastic and metal dishes, equipment for pretend washing and ironing, water play toys, wooden car to ride, large wooden nuts and bolts (large enough not to be swallowed), sand pit, bucket and spade, rocking horse, telephone, playdough, Noah's ark, dressing-up clothes.

2½ to 3 years. Big wooden beads and strings, bubble blowing, simple puzzles, bean bags, large brushes for painting with water colours, wheelbarrow, large cartons and boxes, climbing frame, swing.

Pre-school children. Pre-school children are acquiring skills in building with different materials, handling pencils and paintbrushes, recognizing colours and shapes.

3 to 4 years. Blunt scissors, magazines, etc. to cut pictures from, paintbrushes and paper, large wooden building blocks, planes, fire engines, farm layouts, garages, wooden constructional sets with large pieces, jigsaws with up to 15 pieces, doll with cradle and pram, easel or wall blackboard, percussion and wind instruments.

4 years. Nurse and doctor kits, materials for play shops, Wendy house, small-scale garden tools, trowel and hand fork, doll's house and furniture, jigsaws with 25 pieces, scales, pots and pans, glove puppets, first sewing with bodkin, first wooden letters.

5 years. Materials to draw and paint, modelling materials, playdough, desk and chair, scrap-books, humming tops, table games with dice, card games, picture dominoes, tricycles and pedal cars, large magnet, musical instruments (drums and bells, chime bars), building sets (e.g. Lego), picture construction sets (e.g. Fuzzy Felt).

6 to 8 years. Hammer, saw, nails and wood for simple carpentry, skipping rope, needles and embroidery thread, stilts, space hopper, footballs, dolls, furniture, etc. for doll's house, mechanical toys (e.g. police cars, remote control submarines), knitting.

8 to 10 years. Puppets, construction kits, jigsaws, games, e.g. Equable/Scrabble (the smaller scale Travel Scrabble is often more practical than the standard-sized version), punch ball, printing set, table football, materials for hobbies, e.g. stamp collecting, Master-mind (version for the blind also available), table tennis, chess, draughts (magnetic type), selection of books for all ages, records and record player.

Make-it-Yourself Toys

Many 'homemade' toys can be produced by the staff and children. The play value of these toys is often in the fun of making them as well as the sense of creative achievement they give to the child (see Chapter 6 for ideas). The following items will all be found useful for 'do-it-yourself' toys, and play staff and parents can be encouraged to save them for the playroom stock.

Plastic cartons (e.g. yoghourt and cream)
Egg boxes
Kitchen towel and toilet roll centres
Liquid detergent bottles
Shoe and cigar boxes
Wire coat-hangers
Wire lamp-shade frames
Plastic spoons
Foam rubber pieces
Cotton reels
Unused shelf paper or wallpaper
Carpet squares
Material remnants
Odd pieces of fur
Jam jars
Mail order catalogues
Old Christmas and birthday cards
Silver foil

Suitable clothes, hats, scarves, belts, etc. will be needed for the ward dressing-up box.

OUTDOOR ACTIVITIES

Ideally the children on any children's ward should have access to an open space, either at ground floor level or onto a roof garden. The area should be designed to accommodate a flat surface for play equipment as well as providing space for children in beds, cots or wheelchairs whenever the weather and circumstances permit. The outdoor area should also include some landscape gardening of shrubs and plants. The whole area will need secure fencing to avoid children straying, and to avoid the entry of unwanted intruders. Benches and tables suitable for outdoor use should also be provided for the children, parents and staff.

Play Equipment for Outdoor Activity

Climbing frame. There are various types of climbing frame available; a wooden one, which is collapsible, is probably best, as the frame can also be used indoors. These frames often have a small hinged door and may even include a slide, which increases their versatility and value for the children. The design of the frame lends itself to imaginative play as well as providing an outlet for excess physical energy for those children able to use it.

Equipment for balancing. Narrow planks supported on a line of bricks will provide a base for the child to walk along. This is inexpensive and helps young children to gain confidence when achieving balance.

AGGI-seesaw. The AGGI-seesaw is an entirely tubular construction that can be folded away like an ironing-board.

Tyre on castors. The child lies on his stomach and can paddle himself along with his hands. This is popular with older active children.

Flying saucer. Instead of lying on the tyre, the child sits on it and propels himself around using his feet. This is a useful toy for children aged four to eight, helping them to achieve mobility.

Here the outdoor play facilities include a sandpit, climbing frame and paddling pool.

Play blocks. Play blocks are large but light building shapes made of foam rubber covered in tough, colourful PVC. They are very stimulating for children of all ages and can be used indoors and out.

Play barrel. A play barrel makes a fascinating small hide-out for younger and less active children to crawl into, and provides exciting fun for older ones who can somersault over or jump in it as well as roll and be rolled in it. It is ideal for group play.

Concertina tunnel. Made in a light fabric so as not to be too dark, this toy is very valuable for young children to crawl through. They enjoy the feeling of experimentation of going through from one end to the other.

Land boat. The land boat is a large strongly-made boat-shape on castors. It is very popular for group play and can also be used for sand and water play.

8. Play for Special Children

There are some sick children who have to be cared for in special situations usually because of their clinical condition or handicap, or who need special consideration for the same reasons. These children pose a considerable challenge to the nurse and play worker.

It is in an attempt to help meet this challenge that the following play suggestions are provided for these groups of children. Where appropriate some clinical detail has been given, with a view to helping those working with these children to create more constructive play opportunities designed for the individual child's play needs.

Accident and Emergency Departments

Children coming to accident and emergency departments are acutely ill, often in pain, bewildered, anxious, shocked or distressed and need ideally to be cared for in a separate area of the department (see *Hospital Facilities for Children*, HM(71)22, DHSS 1971). The first priority will always be the appropriate medical treatment which in some instances is life-saving. Opportunities for play will be very limited. However, attractive posters and paintings can be used to add some comfort to the surroundings. In treatment rooms, too, paintings on the ceiling can be seen by the child when he is lying on a trolley or couch. This can also be most helpful during ophthalmic examinations in encouraging the child to fix his eyes on a certain familiar item or character in the painting. There should be some sturdy, bright, but easily handled toys on the window sills for the child to look at and hold. They will also be valuable as part of treatment, e.g. the doctor may listen first to teddy's chest before auscultation of the child's.

Special Care Baby Units

It is easy to dismiss the play needs of babies in special care units. However, even low birth-weight infants need the constant stimulus of encouraging words, songs and nursery rhymes; for as they grow, so they will learn to respond to the mother's or nurse's voice. Later they will learn to focus on, and touch, objects.

Toys and playthings needed at this age are few, but encouraging the mother to play with her baby is most important. Even when tubes and infusions are in place the mother can often be shown how to lift her baby safely without any of them becoming detached. Suitable toys include soft woollen balls or animals, rubber toys and a small rattle.

A regular routine should be established by changing the mobiles hanging above the cot and the toys attached to the cot toy rails (see page 55) to avoid boredom and encourage the child to focus on different objects.

Day Care Wards

An increasing number of children are now admitted to day care wards, either for minor surgery, investigations or treatment. The length of stay is usually no more than 24 hours, often much less. During this time a great deal of medical and nursing attention will be given to the child. Ideally a parent will be present throughout the stay. Toys and play materials provided should involve both the child and his mother, for instance, simple board games, cards, peg boards, dolls, farmyard or garage on a tray, constructional toys, e.g. Lego. Activities provided need to be fairly quiet. Plenty of short story books and albums for all ages should be available. Posters and paintings should decorate the walls.

Out-Patient Clinics

During the course of a year each paediatric out-patient clinic will have hundreds of children passing through and even with a good appointment system some waiting is sometimes inevitable. This leads to the children becoming bored and irritable. Sturdy activity toys should be available for the children to use, e.g. rocking horses, pull-along carts and trucks, a Wendy house, slide and indoor climbing apparatus. There is also a need for a book stand and a 'quiet corner' for some of the children. Posters and paintings should decorate the walls, and these should be changed fairly frequently, perhaps at each new season, to give variety.

A volunteer play worker or member of staff should always be specifically designated to organize play activities during paediatric out-patient clinics.

Intensive Care Units

Children in intensive care units may be recovering from major surgery or road traffic injuries or may require assisted ventilation to maintain oxygenation of the body and its tissues. For whatever reason the child is there, he will be attached to some form of monitoring equipment, intravenous infusions, ventilators or pumps, and will come into contact with many more staff than in the average children's ward.

The child may be unconscious, in which case the nurse should remember that hearing is often the first sense to return on the way to regaining consciousness. The nurse can use this knowledge by speaking to the child in a kindly and reassuring manner when carrying out nursing care such as bathing or treating pressure areas. The nurse should never feel self-conscious about this, and it will be particularly comforting to the parents. Stories can be read and nursery rhymes told. A 'music box mobile' will provide gentle soothing music for short periods at a time or 'pop' music for the teenager. Ward-made mobiles (see page 52) can be hung above the bed where they will not obstruct equipment, but will be bright and gay for the child to see. Colourful posters attached to the walls will add a note of brightness. Ceiling paintings will also help provide a brighter atmosphere.

For the child attached to a ventilator for a long period of time, life must go on. A nursing routine should be devised which meets his need for stimulation and comfort. The presence of the tube will affect speech to some extent, and it is a good idea to have a writing board or slate always available, even for the child who cannot yet read or write, as a great deal can be conveyed with simple line drawings. Although these children often tire very quickly, many play activities are possible. These include finger or hand puppets, which are often very successful, dolls, small aquaria, a wormery (see page 75), growing plants (carrot tops, bulbs, mustard and cress, see page 71), kaleidoscopes, and magnetic games on an adjustable bed-table.

CHILDREN WITH SPECIFIC CLINICAL NEEDS

Children Receiving Intravenous Therapy

Intravenous infusions are widely used in paediatric treatment, sometimes for just a few hours or for several days. The veins most commonly used are those in the arm, although sometimes the foot is used or the scalp in small babies. If the arm is used it should be the one which the child uses least, and the nurse should always remind the paediatrician which one this is. For the child it means being 'one handed' for what may seem to be eternity. To help occupy the child, fullest use of the 'good hand' should be made in play.

Of course a great deal depends upon the age of the child as to his play needs, but the 'Dycem' non-slip mats are most useful for providing a stable base on the bed-table for many activities, e.g. for constructing models with Lego, or for stirring pastry in a bowl. Books should not be too heavy or large as they can be quite difficult to hold with only one useful hand. If available, a book-stand can be invaluable to the child being infused. Care should be taken to ensure that the stand is placed on the child's good side and is within easy reach.

Magnetic games can usually be managed, and card games are possible if a card holder is available; card holders can be obtained through the Red Cross. Posting games, finger painting and potato printing are all possible and will enable the child to use his imagination and creativity.

For the older child wishing to paint the models he has made, an old carving-bench clamp can prove useful for anchoring the item to be painted.

Children with Visual Handicap

Partially sighted or blind children admitted to hospital will require considerable attention and time in order that they can learn to adapt to their ward environment and achieve some independence. Care should be taken by all the staff to avoid placing too many physical restrictions in the way of the child, but obviously everyone must be concerned for the child's safety since he will be unable to see any obstacles in his path.

When he is allowed up the child should be given the opportunity to explore the ward, at first with his mother or his nurse, but as confidence grows, on his own. His bed can be made easily identifiable by wrapping ribbons or sticky tape round the rails at the foot, and his locker by attaching a remnant of carpet or foam rubber to the door and sides; this will also help to develop tactile sense.

Opportunities for developing the senses of touch, hearing and smell must be provided in play in order to compensate to some extent for the visual handicap.

A wide-pocketed apron or coverall can be very useful to the child when playing, providing not only good protection for the child's clothes but also a convenient place for the child to keep precious belongings within easy, safe reach.

The playroom stock should include noisy toys, posting boxes, bricks of varying shapes and materials, and nesting toys, all of which will encourage the child to develop manual dexterity and touch by exploration. Textures are also important. A temporary wall facing can be made with the help of volunteers and other children in the ward, using easily obtainable items. As in making a collage, items of varying textures can be arranged in strips or patterns on the sides of cardboard boxes or stiff brown paper; the child can learn to identify, feel and enjoy the different textures. Suggested items could include:

Stones
Shells
Milk bottle tops
Foam rubber chips (often used in stuffing of toys, etc.)
Various materials cut into strips for hanging (string, old clean nylon tights, leather from old belts)
Cotton-wool balls
Knitting wool twisted into shapes
Carpet oddments
Lino squares and odd tiles
Assorted buttons
Dried beans, lentils and macaroni
Kapok
Kitchen scouring pads or wire wool (not too coarse)
Twigs, straw, bark, cork or pieces of wood, smooth but textured

The nurse will probably think of many more items that can be included. If the wall facing is made in sections, they can be changed during the child's stay in hospital.

Visually handicapped children usually enjoy music and can have great fun joining in a percussion band, especially when the instruments have been made by the children on the ward (see page 66), but Sister will have to be consulted as to the best time for the performance! Bags made from scraps of material and filled with lavender, pot-pourri or pungent herbs will also provide enjoyment of a quieter kind. For a special occasion a herb pillow filled with pot-pourri and covered first with foam lining and then perhaps with velvet on one side and a smooth cotton on the other will give much pleasure.

The Royal National Institute for the Blind (RNIB) (for address, see page 116) sells many adapted forms of the popular children's games, e.g. dominoes and draughts. Older children can be taught the time using the RNIB embossed clock dial. Jigsaws with raised pictures are available from the RNIB; if the jigsaw is kept on a tray the child will be less likely to lose any of the pieces. Talking books can also be obtained, suitable for children aged seven and upwards.

Visually handicapped children should also be given opportunities to take part in sand and water play as well as using playdough and pastry.

Children Nursed in Isolation

Isolation is used for children with an infection, or to protect them from infection (reverse barrier).

The nursing technique varies a little from one unit to another, but essentially those coming into contact with the child will be required to wear gowns, often masks and in some instances caps as well. (A good hand-washing procedure must also be followed.) These gowned figures can be quite frightening for the child, and may increase his feeling of isolation. His mother or father should be given every encouragement to stay, having first been instructed in the appropriate gowning procedure.

Because of the risk of cross-infection, each child should have his own supply of suitable toys for which storage space should be provided in the cubicle. The nurse or play worker should also prepare new toys to take in from time to time to give variety. Before any toys are removed from the cubicle they will require disinfection according to the hospital infection control procedure. Some items, e.g. comics, paper books, etc. may have to be incinerated.

Communication is all-important, and ways must be found to encourage this for the child. The windows of the cubicles should be low enough for the children to look out and for others to look in (attractive curtains can be provided for privacy when needed). A supply of washable felt-tip pens and paints can be provided for the child who is old enough to write or draw messages on the window or on a board, to companions outside the cubicle. Many children become most adept at this. A system of two-way communication can be set up between cubicles using baby alarms, or 'walkie-talkie' sets for the older child, but these are rather expensive. Woodpecker Toys make two wooden receivers (on the cocoa-tin telephone principle) which give excellent voice reproduction along a length of tubing (a garden hose can be used). A 'Talking Telephone' or a discarded GPO telephone can be invaluable for the younger patient. Sometimes the child enjoys dressing up to mime to passers-by and other children; a great deal can be conveyed this way and much enjoyment obtained.

Toddlers often prefer their cot to be pushed up to the corridor window, rather than being in the middle of the cubicle. This allows for hand and face contact against the glass with people in the corridor, and they enjoy its shiny, smooth surface too! Older children can have their cot pushed against the middle cubicle window opposite their next cubicle companion, and some games can be played in this way, e.g. noughts and crosses.

All the normal ward play activities should be possible, taking into account the child's age, condition and the isolation, with the exception of cooking and sand play. Water play can be provided using a plastic washing bowl or portable bath on a stand.

Children in Isolators

The plastic isolator is a metal frame supporting a plastic tent. It is divided into two sections; the patient isolator and the supply isolator. These are connected by a large circular porthole. The tent has large indentations, half-suits in which staff and visitors may enter the patient isolator without coming into physical contact with the totally sterile atmosphere. There are arm-length gloves for reaching into the isolator. All air entering is filtered and the isolator

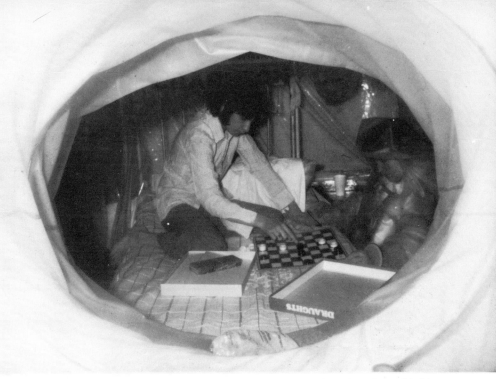

Through the porthole; a child in a plastic isolator is playing draughts with his nurse.

is kept completely sealed. This is absolutely essential as these children are very ill as a result of bone marrow suppression and therefore have no natural mechanism to protect them against infection. The child may be nursed in an isolator for many weeks before and after receiving a bone marrow infusion from a suitable donor.

Everything entering the isolator must be sterile, and as storage space is limited, great thought and anticipation must be shown in the selection of toys for these children. Before being transferred to the isolator the child will have been nursed on reverse barrier precautions for a while; this gives an opportunity for the nurse to discover her patient's particular interests, hobbies, likes and dislikes. Suitable toys and games can then be chosen, packed and labelled prior to autoclaving or gamma irradiation and given to the child on transfer to the isolator. Variety and a surprise element should be included in the choice, as well as the patient's own requests. Paper, pencils, books, puzzles, creative toys, soft toys and construction kits are all suitable. Exercise is important for the child, as he will be confined to a small area for a considerable time. With the cooperation of the physiotherapist daily keep-fit sessions can be organized and some of the other children (and staff) can join in. Television and the radio are much enjoyed and the children often get great support from watching their heroes on the screen.

Preparation for Eye Surgery

Operative technique, and also the subsequent care, will obviously vary from one condition to another. Many eye operations do require, however, that the child's eyes are covered post-operatively for a varying period of time. Correction of squint is the most common eye operation performed. The child is well and active before admission, thus has to cope with separation from home and restriction of physical activity as well as adapt to the strange hospital environment.

The child and his parents should know before operation and, if possible, before admission, that his eyes will be temporarily covered post-operatively. In play before operation the child should be given the opportunity to bandage his teddy's or doll's eyes, as well as experiencing this himself. Bandaging should be done with much reassurance from the nurse and the child given frequent opportunities to repeat the bandaging of his teddy's eyes.

When the child returns from the operating theatre he will be much more cooperative and relaxed as he will know why his sight is affected and will therefore be much less likely to try and pull off the pads. His mother or nurse sitting at the bedside will be able to assure the child that teddy too is there with his eye pads on, which the child will be able to feel for himself. When the pads are finally removed and any eye drops or ointments instilled, the same procedure should be carried out for the teddy and the child can share in this.

Children with Eczema

In the initial stages of eczema it is best to avoid sand and water play. The ward sister will be able to advise when water play can be encouraged. A little Ung. Emulsificans (which helps soften water and gives a slight lather) may be added to the water, making water play even more pleasurable and therapeutic. An alternative method is to place the Ung. Emulsificans on the child's arms before he starts water play. Care must be taken that the arms and flexures are well dried when the child has finished.

Children with Diabetes

Diabetic patients suffer from deficient insulin action caused either by diminished insulin excretion by the islets of Langerhans in the pancreas, or by the presence of insulin antagonists which render any insulin produced ineffective for carbohydrate metabolism.

Once the acute phase of his admission is over, the diabetic child will usually be able to take part in all the ward play activities, but he should also be encouraged to take part in more energetic games and walks outside if these can be arranged. A daily programme planned with the ward sister in cooperation with the parents will enable the child to reach a greater degree of stabilization before discharge home.

A point to remember when the ward play includes pastry-making and cooking is to consult the dietitian about the eating of the tarts or cakes made, as the child's diet may need to be adjusted for that day to allow for their carbohydrate content. As it may be necessary for the child to receive daily insulin injections, opportunities for 'needle play' along the lines suggested by Madeline Petrillo in *Emotional Care of Hospitalized Children* should be given in order that the child understands and integrates the experience. Children from about the age of seven to eight are usually able to understand the need for insulin and its action if the explanation is given in language they can appreciate. It can sometimes be helpful to give the analogy of a motor car needing petrol (carbohydrate = food) and oil (insulin) in order for the engine (body) to run smoothly.

Children with Coeliac Disease

Coeliac disease occurs in children with a sensitivity to gluten found in wheat and rye, which results in a malabsorption state. The child suffers from steatorrhoea (fatty bowel actions), abdominal distensions, irritability and failure to thrive. Treatment basically consists of a diet from which gluten has been omitted.

Modelling is a favourite pastime of some young children, but as they often put things into their mouths, the ward playdough (see page 57) is best avoided for children with coeliac disease. Plasticine should be used instead. In the same way, care must be taken with any ward cooking activities. The usual pastry-making play should be avoided and gluten-free biscuits can be made instead; these will be enjoyed by all the children on the ward. The special flour needed can usually be obtained from the dietitian.

Gluten-free biscuits. The following ingredients will make 30 biscuits:

> 6 oz Rite Diet gluten-free flour
> 3 oz margarine
> $\frac{1}{2}$ egg
> $1\frac{1}{2}$ oz sugar

Method:
1. Rub the fat into the dry ingredients and mix to a smooth paste with beaten egg.
2. Roll out on a board dusted with Rite Diet gluten-free flour or cornflour and cut into desired shapes.
3. Bake on a lightly greased baking tin in a moderate oven for approximately ten minutes or when biscuits are light golden brown. Regulo 3 or 350° F.

Variations. Add $\frac{1}{4}$ tsp cinnamon or 2 oz currants to Rite Diet gluten-free flour and proceed as above.

Children with Hearing Defects

Many children have a hearing problem. A few children are profoundly deaf whilst others have a minimal loss; these conditions may be permanent or temporary. Some of these children can be helped with the fitment of a hearing aid, which they may need to be encouraged to wear and use properly. Hearing is intricately linked with speech and every nurse should appreciate the importance of talking to children, even the very young.

Opportunities for the nurse to talk to her patient occur all the time, during bathing, feeding and bed-making. Care should be taken to use words that the child can understand and always to face the child when talking or reading to him. Avoid using 'baby talk' which will only confuse the child's speech development. Opportunities to encourage speech development in play too are numerous. Nursery songs and rhymes with finger puppet action (see page 49), listening games and 'making music' will all help. Reading books to the child which he can choose from the ward library will encourage his interest and participation in speech (see page 64).

Indiscriminate use of the radio and television in the ward should be avoided since it does little to encourage speech and serves only to produce a cacophony of sound which is distracting to children and staff.

Mentally Handicapped Children

Mental handicap can be defined as inadequate mental development resulting in incapacity for independent social and intellectual adaptation in everyday life. There are many causes for this handicap which can be classified into the following groups:

1. Genetically determined, e.g. Down's syndrome
2. Ante-natal infection, e.g. rubella or syphilis
3. Birth injury or hypoxia
4. Post-natal infection, e.g. encephalitis or cerebral infection

Mentally handicapped children are sometimes admitted to the ordinary children's ward. As with normal children, they vary in much the same way and have the same play needs according to ability, age and interests, but will need more, not less, of the normal childhood pleasures and activities. The child should constantly be praised and encouraged so that he will feel secure and want to do his best.

In order to meet his play needs, the mentally handicapped child must first be taught to play and this should be done as early as possible. Some of these children learn a great deal from imitative behaviour, rather than from curiosity as does the more able child. Some of the less able children need to be taught a great deal, in small stages, slowly and with frequent repetition.

A technique called 'chaining' is a useful tool for playing with these children. It is simply to start from the end and work back slowly, step by step. Wooden inset puzzles are ideal to start with. First show the child the completed picture, talk about it, then take

Mentally handicapped children need opportunities for play, just as do normal children. Here the nurse is ready to help if necessary.

out a piece and put it back. As you show the child each step, get him to repeat it, remembering all the time to praise and encourage him. The aim is for the child to have the achievement at the end of being able to replace all the pieces.

Many mentally handicapped children find it difficult to concentrate or to take any active interest in their environment. It is therefore most important to provide opportunities for each child to take stock of his surroundings, to explore and assess his environment. It is often difficult to keep the mentally handicapped interested in an activity for more than a short space of time. The nurse should therefore be sure to have plenty of equipment with her, to prevent her ideas being quickly exhausted. On the other hand, once an idea has been well accepted it will give satisfaction for a considerable period. Many mentally handicapped children are also physically handicapped, which may make it even more difficult for play to take place. No opportunity should be lost to the nurse to encourage the child's potential to learn. For the very handicapped child who first learns to touch, then grasp and fit a shape in a posting box, it may well be the first step to grasping a spoon for self-feeding.

Every effort should be made to make the child's environment as attractive as possible, with posters and paintings on the walls. Mobiles for hanging which the children can take part in making will all add colour. There should also be plants, flowers and bulbs on the ward for the child to touch, smell and hold.

The child's position should be changed frequently if he is immobile, so that he will come into contact with differing perspectives. A non-ambulant child needs new experiences, of being placed at different heights, for example, on a staged climbing frame, or rolling on an inflatable mattress. Outside activities should be encouraged; feeling the rain on the face and hearing the wind in the trees can be an exciting and enjoyable experience for the young handicapped child.

Children with Orthopaedic Conditions

Orthopaedic conditions cover a wide range, from the child with a fairly simple fracture of a limb, to the child requiring major surgery for scoliosis. Some of these children will be severely restricted in their range of bodily movements for several months. Often, too, they may be attached to some form of mechanical apparatus, e.g. a Stryker frame. Many of them require frequent re-admission for further treatment.

The special play needs of these children are considerable and play must be adapted to their degree of handicap. It is important to provide overhead mirrors in order that the child who has to lie on his back can view himself and the activities going on about him in the ward. Page turners and book-stands too need to be provided; these can be adapted to take a magnetic board, which will enable the relatively immobile child to play several games.

'Play arms' or aids to daily living often used by the elderly and normally obtained through the Occupational Therapy Department

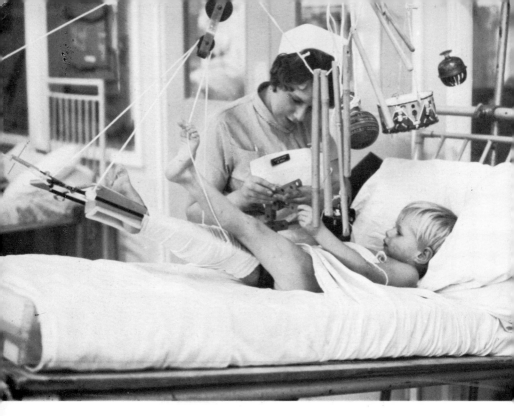

Hanging toys which can be banged and rattled provide entertainment and activity for this young boy with a broken leg in skeletal traction.

will prove invaluable. They allow the child a degree of independence for picking up items that have rolled out of reach.

Many of the ward group play activities can be organized around the bedside of these children, although wherever possible they should be moved into the playroom. It is important that the child, despite immobility, is encouraged to contribute to, and participate in, group activities. Activities of a domestic nature such as cooking and pastry-making are particularly popular.

These longer-stay children often see many other children in the ward going home before they do, and they tend to become discouraged. To help counteract this the child should be given a special responsibility in the ward, perhaps looking after a special plant or choosing records to be played at set times during the day.

Children Receiving Oxygen

Oxygen supports combustion and mechanical toys which may give off a spark should never be given to the child receiving oxygen in any form because of the fire hazard. The nurse should also make sure that the parents and other staff understand the need for this precaution.

Children nursed in oxygen tents usually have some degree of respiratory distress which commonly leads to restlessness and anxiety. The child is only moderately interested in the things about him. Play may only be carried out half-heartedly, toys being picked up and put down again very quickly.

In these situations, the nurse or play worker needs to play for the child, sitting at his side, but only for short periods at a time as concentration is poor and the child tires easily. Puppets with a story are invaluable in this sort of situation, or Play People and their accessories, which the child can easily hold and move about. Any reading books should be light-weight (in size and content). For the baby in an oxygen tent a play cushion (see page 55) in easy reach is a good idea.

THE NEEDS OF ADOLESCENTS

The Report of the Committee on Child Health Services pointed out that 'in recent years it has become increasingly evident that adolescents have needs and problems sufficiently distinguishable from those on the one hand of children and on the other of adults to warrant consideration as a distinct group for health care provision'. The report takes into account the special recreational facilities that this group of patients need.

There are few purpose-built wards for adolescents; the majority of these young people are nursed either in side rooms of children's wards or in adult wards. Wherever they are cared for, facilities must be provided so that leisure pursuits and hobbies may be followed as far as practical.

Most young teenagers have an absorbing interest which usually takes in some form of collecting, e.g. coins, stamps, matchboxes and even railway engine numbers! Every encouragement should be given to allow the patient to pursue and develop his particular

An adolescent patient needs privacy and the opportunity to pursue her interests.

interest. This can sometimes be done by providing books and pamphlets about the hobby.

The hospitalized teenager needs privacy; he also needs the company of his peers and the opportunity to take part in social activities, which are all interlinked. It is self-evident that provision should be made for these needs, although this is not always easy in busy acute hospital wards. However, there is a clear case for not placing these young people with adult patients. A record player with a selection of pop records should be provided for teenage patients to use, preferably in a side room. As the decibel level can be quite high, it may be necessary to provide earphones for the listeners to wear when playing records.

The room of the adolescent in hospital should be kept private. Younger children should only enter by special invitation. Young people particularly need to be on their own at times and this should be respected.

Pin boards should be provided in the rooms for pictures of favourite footballers or pop star posters and other wall decorations.

THE SICK CHILD AT HOME

Whenever possible, sick children should be cared for in their own homes with the help of the family general practitioner, the community nursing services and attendance at the local hospital out-patient department if necessary.

Nursing a sick child at home, however, may tax a busy mother considerably, but her work can be much reduced if she arranges for the child to be on a bed or comfortable settee in the family living-room during the day. Often this also means a ground-floor room with a more interesting view out of the window, a saving in heat and far less expenditure on the mother's energy, with fewer journeys up and down stairs.

Inexpensive Toy Suggestions and Ideas for Play

9 to 18 months. Magazines and comics to tear up, as well as to look at. Simple toys that can be taken apart. Nesting dolls, teddy bears or dolls to dress and undress. Simple rattles made from well-sealed tins filled with pebbles or pieces of wood (this will make just enough noise without deafening the family). Music mobiles.

18 months to 3 years. Old Christmas cards and magazines. Large beads or cotton reels to thread. Building bricks. Small fish tank or budgerigar. A bird table outside the window that can easily be seen by the child (but well away from the family cat). Suitable jigsaw puzzles or picture trays. Conkers, shells, daisies and other flowers to play with and enjoy. Percussion instruments which can be home-made (see page 66). Bowl of warm water and a variety of utensils. Bubbles.

3 to 5 years. Nurse's/doctor's outfit which can be home-made. Glove and finger puppets. Sewing cards and felt cards. Small cars, trains and 'Play People'. Lego or interlocking bricks. Blunt-ended scissors, coloured paper, gummed shapes, scribbling pad, pencils and crayons. Playdough (see page 57). Indoor sand (see page 69). Finger-painting. Potato prints.

5 to 8 years. Mother's button box to tidy (have a supply matchboxes). Knitting dish-cloths for favourite aunts. Embroidery with loosely woven material. Cotton reels with four nails at one end for french knitting. Coloured wool and a blunt needle for stitching mats and bags. Tracing paper and pencils. Books. Kaleidoscope. Magnet with a variety of metal objects from around the house. Furnishing a miniature room using a small empty grocery carton, matchboxes and scraps of material. Cards and Junior Scrabble. A thick notebook to be used for making a diary (words and drawings). Wormery (see page 75).

8 to 12 years. A mirror can give hours of amusement and fun to both boys and girls. Stamps, atlas and a notebook for starting a stamp collection. Construction kits of all descriptions. Jigsaws and games. Cooking, e.g. pastry for tarts, cakes and puddings.

12 to 16 years. Opportunities to follow own hobbies. Record player and pop records (join local library with record section).

A Few Points to be Remembered

Protective covers will prevent undue soiling of the bed.

Supply a good steady surface such as a tray.

Sick children tire quickly, and toys and occupations will need frequent changing.

Big and complex toys tire a child more quickly than small, simple toys which can easily be changed.

A toy enjoyed today may be boring tomorrow.

Toys given for the various age groups will please older or younger children.

The value of any of these toys will be quickly lost if they are left lying around. They should be tidied away regularly to be brought out again another time.

The Toy Libraries Association (see Appendix 3) will be able to provide information concerning the loan of toys, jigsaws, etc.

APPENDIX 1
Reading List and Useful Addresses

General Reading List for Play In Hospital

Child Care and the Growth of Love, by J. Bowlby. Penguin, 1965.

Children in Hospital: The Parents' View, by Ann Hales-Tooke. Priory Press, 1973.

Emotional Care of Hospitalised Children, by Madeline Petrillo and Sirgay Sanger. Lippincott, 1972.

Growing-up, by Catherine Storr. Arrow, 1975.

Hospitals, Children and Their Families, by Margaret Stacey. Routledge, Kegan & Paul, 1970.

Let Me Play, by Dorothy Jeffree, Roy McCorkey and Simon Hewson. Human Horizon Series. Souvenir Press, 1977.

Play, by C. Garvey. Fontana, 1977.

Play, edited by J. S. Bruner, A. Jolly and K. Slyva. Penguin, 1978.

Play and the Sick Child, by Eva Noble. Faber, 1967.

Play in Hospital, edited by Susan Harvey and Ann Hales-Tooke. Faber, 1972.

Playing and Reality, by D. W. Winnicott. Penguin, 1974.

Social Relations and Innovations, by David Hall. Routledge, Kegan & Paul, 1977.

Spontaneous Play in Early Childhood, by Mary D. Sheridan. NFER Publications (Windsor), 1977.

The Lore and Language of Schoolchildren, by I. and P. Opie. Oxford University Press, 1959.

The Needs of Children, by Mia Kellmer Pringle. Hutchinson, 1974.

The Self-Respecting Child, by Allison Stallibrass. Penguin, 1977.

Therapy Through Play, by Ivonny Lindquist. Arlington Books, 1977.

Toys and Playthings in Development and Remediation, by John and Elizabeth Newson. George Allen & Unwin (Penguin), 1979.

113

Working with Children in Hospital, by Emma Clark. Tavistock, 1971.
Young Children in Hospital, by James Robertson. Tavistock, 1970.

Books on Toys and Activities for Children of All Ages

Choosing Toys and Activities for Handicapped Children and *ABC of Toys*. Toy Libraries Association, Seabrook House, Wyllyotts Manor, Darkes Lane, Potters Bar, Herts EN6 2HL.

Fun with Art, by Martin and Cherille Mayhew. J. Galt & Co. Ltd., 1970

Hand Puppets and How to Make and Use Them, by Laura Ross. Worlds Work Ltd., 1971.

How to Make Dolls, by Sylvia Hall. Ladybird Books, 1978.

Making Simple Kites, by Chris Wood. Cassell, 1979.

My Learn to Cook Book, by Ursula Sedgwick. Hamlyn, 1969.

Play Helps: Toys and Activities for Handicapped Children, by Roma Lear. Heinemann, 1977.

Playing Shops, by Evans. Cassell, 1979.

Playing with Fruit and Vegetables, by Sheila Smithson. Cassell, 1979.

Presents for the Family, by Inge Bassingthwaite. Cassell, 1979.

Print, Stick and Stitch, by Carol Walkin and Mary Newland. Cassell, 1979.

Strange Things to Do and Make, by Diana Gribble and Hilary McPhee. Penguin, 1978.

Things to Do, By Hazel Evans. Puffin, 1976.

Things to Make from Card, by Felicia Law. Collins, 1974.

Things to Make from Junk, by Felicia Law. Collins, 1974.

Toys and Ideas for Children when Ill and *Choosing Good Toys for Young Children*. Available free from J. Galt & Co. Ltd., Brookfield Road, Cheadle, Cheshire.

The *Hobby Horse Series* Books 1—6 (Studio Vista) provide numerous play ideas and activities for children of all ages.

Useful Addresses

Association of British Paediatric Nurses,
c/o Miss D. MacCormack, Children's Hospital, Western Bank, Sheffield

Association of Spina Bifida and Hydrocephalus,
Devonshire Street House, Devonshire Street, London W1

British Association of Early Childhood Education,
Montgomery Hall, Kennington, Oval, London SE11

British Epilepsy Association,
Crowthorne House, New Wokingham Road, Wokingham, Berks

British Heart Foundation,
57 Gloucester Place, London W1

British Toy and Hobby Manufacturers Association,
80 Camberwell Road, London SE5 (will supply details of individual manufacturers' catalogues and toys)

Children's Chest Circle,
Tavistock House North, Tavistock Square, London WC1

Coeliac Society,
P.O. Box 181, London NW2

Colostomy Welfare Group,
38 Eccleston Square, London SW1

Diabetic Association,
3–6 Alfred Place, London WC1

Disabled Living Foundation,
346 Kensington High Street, London W8

Down's Babies Association,
Queenbourne Community Centre, Ridgacre Road, Quinton, Birmingham

Family Fund (Joseph Rowntree Social Service Trust Ltd.),
9 Poland Street, London W1 or Beverley House, Skipton, Yorks

Haemophilia Society,
16 Trinity Street, London SE1

Hospital Centre (King Edward VII),
126 Albert Street, Camden Town, London NW1

Ileostomy Association of Great Britain,
149 Harley Street, London W1

Invalid Children's Aid Association,
126 Buckingham Palace Road, London SW1

Leukaemia Society,
116 Torbay Road, Rayners Lane, Harrow, Middlesex

Muscular Dystrophy Group,
Macauley Road, London SW4

National Association for Deaf/Blind and Rubella Children,
164 Cromwell Lane, Coventry

National Association for Gifted Children,
1 South Audley Street, London W1

National Association for Hospital Play Staff,
Thomas Coram Foundation, 40 Brunswick Square, London WC1

National Association for the Welfare of Children in Hospital,
Exton House, 7 Exton Street, London SE1

National Children's Bureau,
8 Wakeley Street, London EC1

National Deaf Children's Society,
31 Gloucester Place, London W1

National Society for Autistic Children,
1a Golders Green Road, London NW11

National Society for Brain-Damaged Children,
Hon. Sec.: 35 Larchmere Drive, Hall Green, Birmingham

Northern Ireland Pre-School Playgroups Association,
84 Donegall Pass, Belfast

Pre-School Playgroups Association,
Alford House, Aveline Street, London SE11

Royal National Institute for the Blind,
224 Great Portland Street, London W1

Royal National Institute for the Deaf,
105 Gower Street, London WC1

Save the Children,
157 Clapham Road, London SW9

Scottish Pre-School Playgroups Association,
Playgroup House, 7 Royal Terrace, Glasgow

The Spastics Society,
12 Park Crescent, London W1

The Toy Libraries Association,
Seabrook House, Wyllyotts Manor, Darkes Lane, Potters Bar, Herts
EN6 2HL

Variety Club of Great Britain,
5th floor, 1–4 Argyll Street, London W1 (gives financial aid to
various charities)

116

APPENDIX 2
Guidelines for Play
Volunteers*

WORKING WITH CHILDREN
IN ACUTE HOSPITAL WARDS

We are pleased to know you are interested to work as a volunteer in our playscheme and we look forward to your joining us. Children are admitted to this hospital because of illness or injury and the care we give them must be the best possible. These guidelines have been compiled to help us all to work together to achieve this.

PLAYING is an essential characteristic of healthy childhood. It is the means whereby a child makes experiments and explores the world, sorting reality from fantasy. It is the way through which he can express to others and to himself, by re-enacting it again and again, what an experience has meant to him. Feelings of love, hope, fear and anger can be safely expressed in play and this contributes to mental health and stability. In hospital, children are often confused, frightened and angry. An adult with time to listen, or with younger ones, simply to hold and comfort them, may help children to manage such overwhelming feelings better. It is the person as much as any particular play activity that is so important at this stage. A playworker in hospital is there to create the setting in which each individual child can find his way to play rather than just to amuse or occupy the children. Play is deeply satisfying, especially when it comes spontaneously from the child himself or is initiated by an adult who understands its true purpose.

* Reproduced by courtesy of THE PLAY IN HOSPITAL LIAISON COMMITTEE, a co-ordinating group representing Save the Children Fund (SCF), Pre-school Playgroups Association and National Association for the Welfare of Children in Hospital, whose aim is the provision of play facilities for all children in hospital.

Volunteers who can help provide the comforting and homely atmosphere which fosters children's ability to play are warmly welcomed in hospital playschemes. Understandably, the organization of play in a busy ward presents special problems if it is to be of real value and support to children undergoing strange and stressful experiences, In addition, volunteers, like regular staff, have special responsibilities in the hospital setting.

This information has been put together to answer some of the questions you may want to ask and to emphasize some of the most important points to understand and accept when working with children in hospital.

1. How to become a volunteer

If you would like to enrol as a volunteer you will be asked to meet the appropriate hospital personnel:

Men and women of all ages are welcome as volunteers. You will of course be able to discuss fully the kind of work you might be asked to undertake. It is usual to have an intro- ductory period to ensure that the arrangements made are mutually satisfactory and this will often include a short course of talks, films, etc. explaining the special needs of children in hospital.

2. Continuity of service

Before making any commitments you should be reasonably certain that you can give several months of regular service. Continuity is of great importance since children and parents as well as staff rely on volunteers, who can become valued members of the ward team.

3. Regular attendance

You will be able to arrange your work according to the hours you wish to give to the hospital service. These arrangements are a commitment to be taken seriously. Reliability is essential. If you do not come when expected the children will feel let down and disappointed. It also causes inconvenience and extra work for the staff. If you are prevented from coming by illness, or any other reason, you should notify the person responsible for the play programme as soon as possible so that alternative arrangements may be made. Make sure you have the correct telephone number to ring (   ).

4. Punctuality

The hospital staff rely on volunteers just as they do on other members of staff so make sure you can arrive on time as arranged.

5. Confidentiality

In the course of their duties voluntary helpers will see and hear matters of a confidential nature. Information relating to the illness, the treatment or the personal affairs of the patient or his family must be treated with the utmost discretion and not discussed inside or outside the hospital, except with those in charge of the child's care. (See Section 17—Duties.)

6. Dress

Suitable clothes are important; ask about this before you join the ward. You may be given a badge or label to help people identify you.

7. Personal belongings

The hospital authorities cannot be responsible for loss of money or valuables. Any loss should be reported at once to the appropriate person.

8. Holidays

Let the ward staff know your holiday dates as soon as these have been arranged so that plans can be made to cover the holiday period. Children and parents too need to know as far in advance as possible when you are going to be away.

9. Smoking

Smoking is not allowed while you are on duty. Canteens used for coffee or meal breaks usually have a section where smoking is permitted.

10. Photographs, slides, films

Photography is not allowed unless prior permission has been obtained from the hospital administrator. If this is given, written permission MUST also be obtained from the parents.

11. Voluntary helpers' visitors
You must always ask the ward sister before bringing a visitor into the ward.

12. Insurance
Before you begin work you should check on insurance coverage for any responsibility you are asked to undertake. It should be noted the the Industrial Injury contributions and benefits are payable only in respect of insurable employment and that benefits cannot be claimed by persons who are injured in the course of carrying out voluntary work in hospitals. It may be possible to obtain insurance cover by joining a voluntary organization already working in the hospital.

13. Health
You should be prepared to have a medical examination and chest X-ray before undertaking work with children in hospital. If you have a cold, sore throat or tummy upset you should telephone the ward sister before coming on duty that day.

14. Fire precautions
Ask the ward sister about the fire safety precautions in the areas where you work and make sure you understand the drill.

15. Expenses
Enquire if the hospital will reimburse travelling expenses which may arise in the course of your work for the hospital. Arrangements can sometimes be made for provision of meals or refreshments without charge to voluntary helpers where the period of duty is long enough. The detailed arrangements are for each district to decide.

WORKING WITH CHILDREN

16. Play responsibility
Responsibility for the general play programme in a ward rests ultimately with the ward sister. If there is a permanent play worker this responsibility will be delegated to her as she provides the continuity so essential for children in hospital. You

should consult her, or, if she is not available, the ward sister, at the beginning of each session so that your help will give maximum benefit. As a play volunteer in hospital you have offered to give help and to put the needs of the children first. You may be asked to set aside your own preferences for a certain child in order to give your warm attention to another whose needs are greater.

It is no easy matter to select the children most needing care but this will be learnt with experience. When a child is particularly distressed or unvisited he may need a great deal of help and other children will find it hard to understand why he is receiving so much attention. Some children seek attention; others withdraw and appear 'good'—this can be a symptom of distress which is easily overlooked. Observe all the children carefully for they may show their distress in many different ways—by facial expression, gesture, in their activity or lack of it. LOOK AT THEM AND LISTEN TO WHAT THEY HAVE TO SAY.

It is important for the children not to lose faith in adults, so in talking to them and in answering their questions never mislead them. Don't be afraid to say 'I do not know—let's ask nurse, or the doctor, or the playworker'. Such questions as 'Am I going to get better?' should always be referred to the ward sister.

Only make promises if you know you can fulfil them, for disappointment will upset the children and may well cause subsequent difficulty for the staff member having ultimate responsibility for the ward play.

During some periods of the day there may be a teacher in the ward providing opportunities for play as part of the children's educational programme. On these occasions, working in close co-operation with the teacher is important. It is in the best interest of the children that ALL who attend the ward work co-operatively.

17. Duties

You may be asked to work in the ward, in the playroom, in cubicles, with individual children or with small groups. Some hospitals also ask volunteers to run play sessions in the Out-Patient Clinic areas or to help a hospital teacher during school hours. It is helpful to know if you prefer working with babies, toddlers, school-age children or adolescents.

The ward sister or the playworker will give you appropriate information about the children with whom you will be working. If you are at all concerned with any aspect of your work or worried about any particular child PLEASE DO NOT HESITATE TO SEEK HELP. There is always a sister or a staff nurse on duty and in many instances a playworker. Ask advice whenever necessary.

18. The volunteer and the child's family

Even while in hospital a child remains a member of his family. Some parents now spend longer periods on the wards caring for their child. They are often under great strain. Always make them feel welcome. Encouraging them to take part in the play programme helps them to feel more at ease and to play more naturally with their own child. Brothers and sisters may also be frequent visitors and should be encouraged to participate in the play activities.

19. Play notebook

It is helpful to keep an up-to-date list in the play notebook in the ward of the names of the different people visiting or working on the ward. If a child becomes attached to a toy and would like it for the next session, make sure that other people concerned know this. Toys to be repaired could also be listed. If there is a register for volunteers, please sign it and if necessary leave a note about any special aspects of your session.

20. Play materials

You will need to know what equipment is available. Whenever you can, let children choose their own activities. When children are engrossed in play they should be interrupted as little as possible. Toys, games and play materials appropriate to ages, needs, interests and condition of the children should be provided. Make sure they have suitable bedtables or trays and can easily reach and use the toys provided. Be careful that all toys given to children and PARTICULARLY TO BABIES are safe and clean. Remember that babies put everything into their mouths and can easily swallow small objects.

The play staff are responsible for the selection, maintenance and storage of play materials. All play materials should be well maintained and toy cupboards should be arranged in such a way that people can easily find equipment as it is needed.

Broken toys should not be replaced in general storage cupboards until they have been repaired (make a note of any in the play notebook—see Section 19). Puzzles should be especially cared for; if one piece is missing the puzzle is ruined. After work, leave the ward or play areas in good order; this is particularly important after messy activities. Remember to clean the equipment, tables and floor and store the play materials systematically at the end of each session. Make sure that a selection of **suitable** toys and activities is left ready and available at all times for children of any age.

21. Evening volunteers

Quiet activities are more suitable for the evening. If children become excited it is difficult for them to settle down at night.

SPECIAL PRECAUTIONS

22. Reporting accidents.

Accidents, however small, e.g. slipping and falling on wet floor, catching fingers in cupboards, pricking fingers, etc., should be reported to the sister or nurse in charge of the ward at the time. Always ask if a written record is required.

23. Food, sweets and drinks

It is essential that food, sweets and drinks (including water) should not be given to any child without the permission of the sister or staff nurse in charge of the ward. Food, sweets and drinks should not be left within reach of the children, some of whom might be on a special diet, having fluid measurement or be about to have an anaesthetic before an operation.

IT IS VERY DANGEROUS TO EAT OR DRINK BEFORE HAVING AN OPERATION. IF THIS WERE TO HAPPEN UNKNOWN TO HOSPITAL STAFF IT COULD CAUSE SERIOUS HARM.

24. Infection

This can spread easily in a children's ward and extra care is required to ensure that toys which a child may have had in his mouth are not passed on to another child before being cleaned.

Isolation cubicles. There are special techniques, including wearing a gown and mask, to prevent the spread of infection. The ward sister will explain these to you if you are asked to play with a child in isolation. Planning what toys and activities are safe and suitable in these circumstances will need careful thought and discussion with the staff.

25. Bedpans, toilets, nappies
Volunteers should check on individual children before taking on this responsibility and ask permission before taking children to the toilet as tests may be in progress. It is useful to know the children's own words for the toilet.

26. Moving and transporting children
Children who have had operations may need lifting in a special way—always ask about this.

Children must not be taken from the ward or playroom without permission from the ward sister. Similarly children must not be taken from bed or cot without permission.

27. Other important safety measures
If you play with a child who is in a bed or cot and you lower the side, ALWAYS RAISE AND FASTEN IT SECURELY before you leave the child.

CHILDREN IN A PLAYROOM SHOULD NOT BE LEFT UNSUPERVISED.

These guidelines have been prepared by the Play in Hospital Liaison Committee in consultation with the Department of Health and Social Security, the Department of Education and Science and Her Majesty's Inspectorate, the British Paediatric Association, the Association of British Paediatric Nurses and the National Association of Voluntary Help Organizers.

Copyright: © *PHLC 1978.*

Copies of the Guidelines may be obtained from:

NAWCH, Exton House, 7 Exton Street, London, SE1 8UE.
SPPA, Playgroup House, 7 Royal Terrace, Glasgow, G3 7NT.
NAWCH (Belfast), c/o Mrs H. Allen, 12 Carnamena Park, Castlereagh, Belfast 6.

APPENDIX 3
Toy Libraries Association

Toy Libraries initially catered for the needs of physically and mentally handicapped children as well as mentally handicapped adults. Today they open their doors to all children with special needs so that they may benefit from playing with, and borrowing from, a selection of carefully chosen toys. A lonely child is often an unhappy child and a Toy Library provides children with an opportunity to meet and play with other children in an exciting but caring environment.

Others too can benefit from belonging to a Toy Library. The brothers and sisters of the handicapped child are welcome. There are those with less obvious (although no less real) problems such as families suffering from emotional or social stress. There are groups of people such as childminders and foster parents who seek the advice, and benefit from the help, that a Toy Library is able to offer.

A Toy Library provides good quality (and sometimes specially adapted) toys which may be borrowed and taken home to extend the children's enjoyment and therapy. It is also a meeting point where parents, volunteer helpers and professional advisers can meet informally. Problems are shared, ideas exchanged and many family friendships are made.

Many good quality toys are expensive and so parents, if they can afford to, hesitate to buy in case their child does not enjoy them. A Toy Library gives the parents and child a chance to experiment with a wide selection of toys. Then favourites can be bought with confidence.

The Aims of the Association

The object of the Association shall be the relief and education of all handicapped children by the provision of therapeutic, educational and stimulating toys and equipment, and in furtherance of such an object the Association shall aim:

1. To further the setting-up of charitable independent Toy Libraries in this country, whose purpose shall be
   a. To assist the development from the earliest age of all handicapped children, whatever their disability, in the towns or areas covered by each of them.
   b. To provide the best available toys to them.
   c. To provide an opportunity for professional involvement in a voluntary service for handicapped children.

2. To foster the understanding of the play needs of handicapped children and to give guidance on the selection of good toys and play materials.

3. To promote, work for, and maintain communication between
   a. Individual Toy Libraries
   b. Professional workers and Toy Libraries
   c. Manufacturers, designers and other interested bodies and societies for the handicapped, and Toy Libraries

How to Locate your Nearest Toy Library

Write to the Toy Libraries Association, Seabrook House, Wyllyotts Manor, Darkes Lane, Potters Bar, Hertfordshire, EN6 2HL. The Toy Libraries Association will provide you with the address of your nearest Toy Library (as it is a charity, please remember to send a stamped addressed envelope). It will also give you invaluable advice on how to start a Toy Library in your own neighbourhood if the established library is inconveniently situated.

The Toy Libraries Association also organizes training programmes for those interested in setting up a Toy Library and will provide on request an initiation pack full of information and ideas about the actual mechanism of founding a local Toy Library in a area where one does not already exist. Membership of the Toy Libraries Association can be either as an individual, or as a Toy Library or as a commercial concern. Membership for those living overseas can also be obtained.

Publications

The Toy Libraries Association produces many useful booklets and other publications. Details of these may be obtained from the Association.

Index

1390(S)